The *Julie Rowe* Show

Volume One

Podcasts 1 through 10

The Julie Rowe Show

Volume One

Podcasts 1 through 10

Hosted by Eric J. Smith

spring creek
BOOK COMPANY
Rexburg, Idaho

ISBN 13: 978-1-944657-02-4

e. 1

Published by:
Spring Creek Book Company
PO Box 1013 • Rexburg, ID 83440

www.springcreekbooks.com

Cover design © Spring Creek Book Company

Printed in the United States of America
Printed on acid-free paper

Table of Contents

Podcast 1: Wasatch Wakeup and "The Big One". 1

Podcast 2: Signs in the Heavens #1. 17

Podcast 3: Spiritual Gifts 27

Podcast 4: Overpowering Evil. 44

Podcast 5: Getting to Know Julie Rowe 60

Podcast 6: What I See in the Western United States 81

Podcast 7: What I See in Southwestern U.S.. 100

Podcast 8: The Gathering and GTRF. 113

Podcast 9: Learning of Christ. 133

Podcast 10: The Gathering: Safety in the "Callout" 150

Bonus Section: The Doctrinal Significance of the Callout. . . 165

Acknowlegments

❦

Julie and Eric wish to thank the many people who transcribed these podcasts. Their dedicated efforts are greatly appreciated.

They also express their thanks and gratitude to their spouses and children who have made many sacrifices to allow these recordings to be completed.

PUBLISHER'S NOTE

The original transcripts of these podcasts were carefully prepared by our team of transcribers. Essentially every sound made by Julie, Eric, and the guests was included. For the sake of readability and continuity of the text, many repetitive phrases have been removed, along with most of the verbal responses that weren't tied directly to the message.

In other words, this book series isn't designed to be a "read along" with the podcasts. Some of the paragraphs have been tightened up to make Julie's message more concise and clear. Also, long segments of dialogue have been divided into paragraphs where it was appropriate.

In a few instances where Julie's descriptions of events or doctrine were cut short or incomplete, she has been consulted to clarify what she intended to say.

Podcast 1

Wasatch Wakeup and "The Big One"

Julie Rowe: I'd like to welcome anybody who's listening today. This is our first podcast for the Julie Rowe Show. I'm gonna start in a rather simple interview fashion. I've got my friend Eric on the line and he is helping me with these podcasts as we go forward.

I appreciate those who are listening and your patience as we try to figure this out. This is very much out of my comfort zone, but I'm just feeling that I need to be a stronger voice of warning and make myself more available with this message to reach as many people as possible in serving as a voice of warning, testimony, witness, and truth.

Having said that, I just wanted to again thank you for joining us, and I encourage you to share this with your friends and family members that might have interest in this message.

I have requested of those people who interview me that I do not know what the questions are beforehand. I feel I do better with more of an impromptu format so that I can have, if you will, live stream from the other side as far as the Spirit guiding me in what I'll say.

The interviewers that we have going forward on these podcasts will prepare questions that they find of interest. We'll try to stay within a certain theme or topic, but we are following the Spirit on

1

this and we're just going with where the conversation goes. I want it to be as natural as possible. So with that, I'm going to turn the time over to our host Eric Smith.

Eric: Thanks, Julie. In the time that I've followed your story over the last couple years, I've become interested in the topic of the Wasatch Wakeup. You were on Bryan Hyde's radio talk show on May 5th of 2016, and that was when I really first started hearing that phrase "Wasatch Wakeup." I wanted to ask you where that phrase came from.

Julie: The term Wasatch Wakeup is one that I coined. It has since picked up momentum in the last year or so. That is the phrase that was given to me in both dreams and visions from the other side of the veil. I first heard it in a night vision, and then I had some other day visions regarding the Wasatch Wakeup, which is the first earthquake that will be a wake-up call centered in Salt Lake City, Utah.

I can't take credit for that phrase, since it was given to me from those on the other side of the veil, letting me know that we have some things coming in the very near future. That Bryan Hyde show last year was the first time I was given permission to use that term on a broad scale.

Regarding that earthquake, I typed up a blog entry on **julieroweprepare.com** that is entitled *The Wasatch Wakeup* in April 2016. I encourage anybody who's listening to this to go to there and read my own personal account, and not what's been spread around as rumors on the internet.

There are a lot of rumors that have gone on about my message, my background, and my health issues. I look forward to doing some podcasts to dispel some of those rumors and to let people hear my own voice.

I went public with my story starting in May 2014 when my first book came out, *A Greater Tomorrow*. My second book, *The Time is Now*, came out in November 2014. My third book, *From*

Tragedy to Destiny came out in March 2016, and I am getting ready to publish my autobiography. I don't have a release date on that yet but Eric helped write that, and he is who is interviewing me today.

After being in the public spotlight now for three years, I've had interactions with many people. I'm finding that the more vocal I get and the more bold I am with this message, the more opposition there is, and the more false rumors and other personal attacks have come.

One of the reasons we're doing these podcasts is for clarification on the Wasatch Wakeup, as well as various topics as we go forward. I will address some of the things that I didn't cover in the books, and in doing these podcasts, whoever might be interested in listening can hear my voice and hear the authenticity in this message. While those who oppose this message are doing everything they can to discredit me, I do want to witness and testify that I know the Wasatch Wakeup is real.

I stand by that with every message I've given, whether it's a radio show, a podcast, a book, or anything I have personally written on my blog, or anywhere else on the internet. I stand by those words. Just because I don't explain them doesn't mean they're not correct or that I have changed my story.

I don't always have all the details correctly, because I can only give what I know at the time. My understanding three years ago was a lot different than what my understanding is today. My understanding even a year ago is much different than it is today. I still don't *exactly* know when the earthquake's gonna be, but I was given the words to speak on Bryan Hyde's show a year ago, and I felt an extreme urgency in that message.

I was specifically told by the Lord, or from His messengers on the other side of the veil, primarily John, who I talk about in my book. We could have an entire podcast just on my friendship with John, who is a distant ancestor of mine that is mentioned in my first three books.

Eric: Is John still active in your life?

Julie: Very much so. We'll address that on a different podcast, because that's a whole other topic. One of the many reasons I can do this work is because I know without a doubt that the Lord's hand is behind this message. The more involved I get in it, the more clear it becomes, and the more determined I am to speak boldly and testify of the Savior Jesus Christ and of His mission, which is the gathering of our Heavenly Father's children home.

As one of His messengers, I made a commitment in premortality and again many times while here on this earth. This is not something that you just jump into without knowing what you're getting involved in. I didn't entirely know everything, but I was pretty well prepared from those on the other side, through personal revelation, dreams, visions, and sometimes visitation from those on the other side.

I agreed to it, and at any point in time I can say: "I'm done, I'm not doing any more of this." But in my heart I know that the Lord loves His children. I love my brothers and sisters, and I would never be able to live with myself if I did not do everything in my power to be able to warn and testify to bring as many people back to Christ as possible and to save as many lives as possible. Whether that's spiritually or temporally speaking, and that includes the Wasatch Wakeup.

I did get a bad rap last summer, and I knew that I would. It came as no surprise to me. If someone's gonna claim that she has spiritual gifts and of being able to see the past, present, or future—which is my claim and which I stand boldly by—then it is common sense that she would be shown at least a portion of how she's going to be treated for saying such things.

That is no small claim. It's gonna ruffle feathers and make some people uncomfortable and afraid. They're gonna think I'm a freak, and they're gonna call me crazy. Then coupled with some of the health issues I have, I don't blame people one bit for not believing my story. But I would ask that you visit my website and read my books before you criticize me.

Find out for yourself from the actual source, rather than from negative things on the internet, or gossip and rumors from your neighbors or family members. That's what I would hope for anyone who is seeking truth. That's how we avoid deception. I don't believe everything I read on the internet, and no one else should either.

Eric: Right.

Julie: I think it'd be interesting to hear your perceptions of what was going on in the world at the time of the radio show. What was happening in Utah or the western states where this Wasatch earthquake is gonna affect people on a grand scale?

Eric: Well, I was more active in social media back then than I am now, but I was on some social media groups who were talking about events that were coming. At that time there was a lot of anticipation about things that might happen. That earthquake had been mentioned, and I remember after your radio show with Bryan that the social media websites started buzzing. There was a lot of talk: "Oh, did you hear what she said?"

You were so descriptive in that earthquake. I knew you were describing the events that would happen, such as it would be a certain time in the morning, and you saw snow and grass. You were so descriptive, and I remember thinking, "You don't just make this stuff up."

So I really believed you had been shown that. I really felt like I would see that event in the next couple weeks. When it didn't happen as you had described, for a little while I started getting a little shaky, but I held my convictions that you had seen what you said you saw.

I just had to put it on a shelf for a little while, because I didn't know what to do with it. Since then, I've come to know that it's still gonna happen. We just don't have the certainty on the date, and that's okay.

Julie: Right. Other than within my smallest circle, I've never discussed dates. I have a handful of friends and people on my board that I have surmised that there might be dates. Since my NDE I first saw that and then the first time I remember that they showed me the specifics as far as certain neighborhoods, and the weather.

All that I remember where I got kind of close up views, the first time I saw that was like the fall of 2013. I saw it in vision several times before I actually went public in telling anybody that so I knew with the sequence of events what to look for roughly speaking.

I do get dates on quite a few things, but I have never been given a date on the Wasatch Earthquake specifically. I've been shown times and seasons. I've been shown surrounding events or dominos that will fall before and after, and sometimes during. I have asked for a date on that earthquake , and what I'm being told is they're not gonna give it to me because they know I would wanna tell people!

The Lord doesn't tell us anything that's not good for us and so He's holding that back. I ruffled some feathers at that interview with Bryan Hyde because one of the first things I said in the beginning—and I was prompted to say it by John, very specifically, so much so that it caught me off guard.

Some people have a hard time that I would even claim I have guidance from someone on the other side, or that I hear voices. For that alone they will want to stone me, saying I'm either a false prophet, and others will say, "She's just flat-out crazy because she's admitting she's hearing voices."

I want to be very clear, that there are different ways that we receive revelation. When I first got on that radio show and Bryan turned the conversation over to me, the first thing I heard from the other side was, "Julie, before you go into conversation about the Wasatch, you need to let them know that the Lord does give dates."

Then while on the phone, a vision opened and I was reminded of Samuel the Lamanite and how he was specifically given a date and told that the Savior would come at a certain time. He testified of that for five years, and just before they were going to put all the believers to death, he pled with the Lord again, after having pled for five years many times, he pled with the Lord again and the Lord said, "Fear not, for I come tomorrow."

That's exactly what happened. They opened that vision up to me again and I said, "I wanna be very clear that the Lord does give dates," but I didn't qualify it. I never said, "He's given me a date on the earthquake."

My energy was of such that it was very immediate, it was very urgent, and the words were then given, "The earthquake is imminent."

So it was the combination of that phrase, combined with "imminent."

Then people on the internet were making up all kinds of things that I've said. They were trying to say that I'd posted things on different forums that I hadn't. People don't wanna believe this, but there are people out there pretending to be me. Why would they want to pretend to be me? If they knew my life, they would not want my life. I don't know why they'd wanna pretend they're me.

Eric: (laughs)

Julie: They're pretending on avatars online and they're gonna increasingly do that. They will have imitations of Julie Rowe. Sounds ridiculous, doesn't it? But they've done it already and we haven't seen anything yet. So, there were things that people claimed that I said that I never did say.

But I will own that I did say the Lord does give dates. He gave me the dates for every speaking engagement I had. He gave me the dates, sometimes, for conversations I needed to have with certain people. He's given me dates for when I need to travel to certain locations and work on the relief fund. But He has never given me a date for the earthquake. And I never claimed such, did I?

Eric: No, and I'm just speaking from my own experience here.

I heard some people take that word you used, "imminent," and put their own time scales on it. Like some people mentioned that it would be three days. Then they said, "See, it didn't happen within three days, so she was wrong." We put our own timelines on it.

Julie: That's so funny, because in the eternities, time is not kept the same way at all in the heavens. Not even close. So it's really silly of us to try to put a time on the definition of "imminent." That's just the best word I could come up with that was given to me: "Say imminent."

I heard "imminent" more than once. I had never said "imminent" before on any radio show, and that was purposeful. I think the Lord did want people to be urgent, and He wanted people to be serious about the message.

He wanted to see where their hearts were, and what they were gonna do with the message when He said to them, "imminent." I even said in that broadcast: "That could be a day, it could be next week, it could be next month, it could be next year. But it is imminent."

Here we are a year later and it hasn't happened yet, but I still say to you: It's not only imminent, it's right around the corner.

Eric: Well, time will tell. I mean, in the grand scheme of things, if the world has had mankind on it for 7,000 years, what's a day, a week, or a year, right?

Julie: That's pretty imminent to me. I do know with what's going on in the world, politically speaking, internationally, and nationally, and with other natural disasters going on around the world that they have shown me, we are not any less imminent than it was a year ago. In fact, it's right around the corner. I don't know how soon, but, that urgency hasn't gone away from me.

I have always felt like it was a spring earthquake. For a while I did think maybe I'd gotten it wrong and we were gonna have it in November because I was feeling so much urgency last November.

I was having a lot of anxiety about the fact that so many people had rejected my message or had decided not to believe that I was a true messenger anymore because the earthquake hadn't happened.

That is the reason I did that second Bryan Hyde interview in November, because when you see people struggling in their faith or losing their faith, it's discouraging. I didn't want to be responsible for that.

I wanted to let people know that I still stand by this message. I've seen what I've seen. I'm not backing down from that. This isn't an ego thing. I'm convinced because I'm convinced Christ gave me those messages, and He continues to give those messages to me.

I can't sleep at night if I'm not doing everything I can to warn my brother and sisters. That's how serious this stuff is that's coming to this planet, and it starts with the Wasatch Wakeup.

Every time I speak out like this I get hate mail and things circulate on the internet, but I can't care what people say anymore. It hurts my heart, but it will not stop me and it will not shut me up, because I know who I work for. I'm going to be very clear that I work for the Lord Jesus Christ. When you know who you work for, you know He's protecting you.

Those who are closest to me know how imperfect I am. His pattern is to choose imperfect people. If I were perfect, I wouldn't be on the planet anymore. But He's giving me an opportunity to learn and to grow, just like He is everybody else. I'm so thankful for that, and it's very humbling. I just want to be worthy of His word, worthy of His message, and worthy of returning home to the Savior and to my Father in Heaven. If I've done that at the end of the day, my life is a success.

At some point in time in our lives, we have to look in the mirror and say, "Who's side am I on? If I'm truly on the Lord's side, then what am I willing to do to stand for Christ?"

Many of us are going to be called to do some very difficult things. If I can be one face in the crowd that stands and says, "I'll do whatever He asks me to do," then maybe others will be willing to do the same.

Eric: That's great. I know that your stance has helped me and a lot of others make the same kind of stance to choose the side they're on. So Julie, I want to ask you about the doctrinal background and purpose of the Wasatch Wakeup.

Julie: That's a great question, because this is not coming from me. I'm not creative enough to come up with this. I am by no means a brilliant person. I've been blessed with a sharp mind that has often been inflicted with terrible pain and health issues and other things. So anybody that knows me, my health history and my family background would understand the context I'm giving here.

I did not come up with this on my own. You cannot make this stuff up. I really would have to be one hundred percent completely crazy, or I have to speak the truth. Because it's one or the other.

I don't think there's a lot of gray area in understanding my message, which is that the Lord has a plan for us and He wants us to be happy. We need to trust in His plan, and then we will find safety in that.

The understanding that I have about the Wasatch Wakeup is that it's the beginning of the tribulations spoken of in the Book of Revelation, in Isaiah, and other passages of scripture. It is essentially the first domino or the tipping point of the tribulations. From then on, we have seven years of tribulations, specifically spoken of in the Book of Revelation by John.

Eric: I think that covers it, but are people gonna be hurt? Are buildings gonna be destroyed?

Julie: Absolutely. I see several deaths. I see thousands of people displaced in this first earthquake.

Eric: Then why does the Lord allow this to happen?

Julie: He allows it because upon His housetops He will cleanse

His church first. That's the first thing that comes to mind. The second thing is that He is a God of tender love and mercy. When He sees His children not paying attention, not respecting Him, not obeying His laws and covenants that He has given us for our safety and our protection, then the Lord takes it upon Himself to wake people up.

We often don't listen to the Lord until we're humbled, and that's a sad fact about human nature. That isn't to say that everyone who's gonna be injured or have something negative affect on the Wasatch Front did something wrong. There are plenty of people who are not guilty of anything, who are just good people, but they must endure trials and suffering for their own learning and growth on an eternal path.

It is similar to the days of Noah, when the Lord flooded the earth with water. He cleansed the earth because the earth had gotten so wicked that it was more of a tender mercy for Him to stop them from their own condemnation, than it was for Him to let them continue to go down the path of darkness.

Life continues on the other side of the veil. It's not like you die and no longer exist. You go to the other side of the veil and keep moving on in your progression. Does that answer it?

Eric: That's a good answer. While we're talking about earthquakes, there's a scripture in Revelation 6:12-17. In short it says, "I beheld when we had opened the sixth seal and lo, there was a great earthquake and the sun became black and the moon became blood." He's talking about a really big earthquake there. Is that the same as the Wasatch?

Julie: I'd have to go back and read those passages to know the full context, but my understanding is that we've got huge earthquakes going on all over the planet, but this one in the Wasatch signifies the first domino of the tribulations beginning as we enter into a new dispensation.

The largest earthquake in the Wasatch will come later. It will be a 9 to 9.5, even a 10 on the Richter scale. That one will also be centered in the Salt Lake Valley, splintering out into the rest of Utah. That one does not happen until right after the foreign troops come to the United States. I see that as a fall earthquake.

This first one I see as a spring earthquake, because that one has spring green grass, it's got a fresh snow. The weather is unseasonably warm with an unexpected cold front that comes in for that Wasatch Wakeup. I was even given the times that the first shakes would happen while it was dark, between 4:00 and 4:30 a.m. Then the aftershocks last until 6:00 or 6:30 in the morning before people come out of their houses.

There are specific things on my blog that I talk about, which leads to so much hoopla around my story and why it goes viral throughout the world. I have given these details in a way that no one else has, and people have a buzz about that. They're perplexed, curious, and frustrated. Some of them are very angry and scared.

I think that's where a lot of it comes from. People are scared about who I am. They don't understand how I can know these things. I can't answer that other than to say, I am who I am, and I'm not going to hide from it anymore.

Back to the first earthquake. There's gonna be aftershocks. When you have an earthquake that's a 6.6 to a 7.0, you have to expect aftershocks, right?

Eric: Those are big. Those are the kind that usually knock things off walls and cause structural damage.

Julie: Especially some of those brick buildings that are older and were not structurally built for an earthquake. Also, at Thanksgiving Point and all along I-15 in the Wasatch corridor, I can't tell you how many buildings have been made out of glass, most of them between four and six stories. I have gone there a couple of times a year over the last five years, and I cannot believe they are building those things.

Eric: As you drive past them, do you see specific buildings in a damaged condition?

Julie: Yes. The way it works with the visions I have is that it's as if I'm there experiencing it. The glass is breaking right in front of me, and the roads are breaking up. It does play tricks in my mind. Try driving down I-15, having a conversation with somebody and then having a vision open up to you where you see people falling into a crevice!

I have to actively work at staying in present time. I have grounding techniques that I do. Anybody else who experiences this doesn't tell anybody because they're afraid that someone will think they're crazy. But when you experience gifts like this, there are different techniques that I've been taught how to do to make sure I stay centered and grounded.

Eric: So, you're not actually seeking those experiences? They just kind of happen?

Julie: They just come. It can happen when I'm in a car and somebody asks me a question. All of a sudden it will open up to me and I can give an answer. Often it catches me off-guard. I handle it better than I used to because I understand what's happening. It's a lot better now than when I was six.

But I came into the world like this. I've dealt with this my whole life, and sometimes it plays out like a live video feed. Other times it's a deja vu experience, or I will see something in advance and it will come to fruition. I just don't always have a time frame for when that's gonna happen, though.

I have dreams and visions that I had a decade ago that are just now coming to fruition. I didn't know ten years ago that they were gonna happen when I was 44, I just knew that it was gonna happen someday. In some cases I don't know if it will happen until it actually happens. Then I say, "Wow, that was literal."

Sometimes I think I'm still trying to discern the things that they're teaching me that are just figurative, but other times it's very clear that it's something that's really gonna happen. So when it comes to things like the Wasatch earthquake, there will be aftershocks that same day and a few days later and a few weeks later. Some of those earthquakes are gonna be decent sized. You're gonna have at least a 3.5 to a 4.0, maybe even a 5.0 in aftershocks in the year following the Wasatch earthquake.

Then that Big One happens, which I have confirmed through the Spirit. I first saw that one in vision when I was a kid, but I was a junior in high school when they made clear to me it would be in Salt Lake, Wasatch and Utah County.

I was sixteen as a junior in high school, and I didn't live in Utah. I lived in northern Virginia near Washington D.C. So it's not like I was from there. It was set in such a scene that I saw multiple temples, which are now all built. Every single one of the temples that I saw in 1990 now exists in Utah.

Eric: That's cool.

Julie: So you can imagine how many times they've shown those scenes to me, and the different scenarios of that really big earthquake. It's that important. The Lord started making it clear to me at the age of sixteen years old. That's a lot of training I've had, and you don't mistake seeing things like that.

I saw that big earthquake and thousands of people killed. They were running in horror because they were not prepared or they were caught off guard because they were not listening to the Prophet, or another message where they could have been spared. There's a reason I'm as enthusiastic about this message as I am. I've seen that big earthquake probably once a week for twenty-five years.

Eric: Oh really? What about the first Wasatch earthquake. How many times would you say you've seen that?

Julie: For several years, through my late teens, early twenties and even until I was thirty one. I thought it was all the same earthquake. I wasn't able to discern that it was two different earthquakes for a long time. Then when I had my NDE, they made it very clear, "These are two separate earthquakes."

In the last three years I've seen that Wasatch Wakeup anywhere from once a week to five times a week, and that happens in both night vision and day vision. I believe that's because for my mission I need to stay motivated and have the courage to do what I'm doing. I need to not be afraid and to be compelled to help wake up as many people as possible. Even if it just means they've got a flashlight and a pair of shoes by their bed, or they've taken the mirrors off their walls that are gonna hit them on the head and knock them out.

I mean, I can't save everybody. That's not my job. If somebody's gonna die, then that's their plan and they go to the other side. If someone's gonna get hurt, they're gonna get hurt. But through my actions I hope that people will at least be aware and hear, more than anything, that no matter what happens to you, God loves you.

Eric: Let me ask you another quick question in regard to the timing or at least the sequence of those events. So you see the Wasatch Wakeup as potentially a spring event. And then do you see the big one in the same year, or do you see it like a year later?

Julie: The earliest that the big earthquake could come would be the fall of 2018. At the very earliest, but after the Wasatch Wakeup.

The thing is, people in America have not lived through a 6.5 or a 7. They don't have context. There is no one living in America that has ever gone through that. There are people that have gone through large earthquakes while living or visiting other countries. But on American soil there has not been a 7.0 in a long time.

So the first one is going to come across like the Big One. There will be headlines. People will probably even make T-shirts saying: "I survived the Big One." Because to them, a 7.0 is big, but they haven't lived through a 9.0.

Eric: That's interesting. As you were talking about being a younger girl having dreams and visions, you reminded me of an interview where you told me some stories when you were younger. I think it would be a fun podcast to talk about some of the natural events you saw as a girl. What do you think?

Julie: That would be great. We can talk about Mt. Rainier and Mount St. Helens and some of the other volcanoes like Kilauea. We could even talk about hurricanes and some of that stuff.

Eric: Well, we've pretty well covered this topic. Is there anything else you wanna say?

Julie: I think this is good for today. Again, I don't know the date on this earthquake, but the verbiage given to me is it's right around the corner. The visual that comes with that is that you're walking on a street corner and you're about to turn the corner. So if we are right around the corner, we are at the corner of the street. That's all folks.

Podcast 2

❧

Signs in the Heavens #1

Julie: Hi folks, we'd like to welcome you to the Julie Rowe Show today. This is our second podcast recording. Bear with us as we get used to this system and try to get a few things figured out. I'd like to welcome our guest today. We have my friend Brandon on the line.

Brandon: Hello!

Julie: Hi Brandon! Good to hear from you! We also have Eric here, who is guiding the conversations with us. We'd like to thank him for his work. How you doing Eric?

Eric: Doing great.

Julie: Great. This is our second podcast and the first time that we're doing a three-way call, so we are branching out into new horizons here. We will try really hard not to talk over each other, and I'm gonna try hard not to dominate the conversation too much.

In that first podcast, I felt like the energy was strong and bold, but every podcast will be a little different depending on the topic. I'll open it up to Brandon for his questions today, and the topic of his choice. As mentioned in the first podcast, I prefer not to really know what the topic is gonna be. That way I can essentially have a live stream from the other side of the veil as I receive personal revelation of what the Lord would have me say. So having said that, Brandon, I turn the time over to you to explain what your topic selection is for today.

Brandon: Okay. We know that our God is a God of intelligence, and there's many meanings to that. That also means that He is a God of science, and I would even say the perfect scientist. We understand that eventually all truth will be circumscribed into one greater whole, and true faith and true science will one day intersect. So it was along those lines that I wanted to ask you a few questions regarding the cosmos. Joseph Smith hinted a lot about the cosmos in his life, and how the significance of our faith goes far beyond our human understanding.

In the Book of Moses we get a glimpse of the vastness of creation, and the reason I wanted to get into this is because we have some very interesting events coming up. The solar eclipse is very significant, and in September, the alignment of the planets and some of the constellations are very significant in regard to the New Testament. What can you add to that?

Julie: I love this topic. I love science, and I love what you have shared with us already. One of the reasons I love this topic is because we are on the cusp of some new changes coming into our universe, upon our planet, and around our planet.

With my dad being in the military and us moving around when I was growing up, I think I'm the only one of my siblings that never took a class that studied the stars, although I was always fascinated by it. So I don't have a scientific background on this. Everything that you hear me say has been taught to me either through my NDEs of through dreams and visions, with the exception of a little bit online.

I'm one who can look up into the stars and not recognize anything other than the Big Dipper, basically. I couldn't tell you the names of the constellations or the names of the planets that are passing by. I can recognize a lunar eclipse, and I can recognize the phases of the moon. When I got my teaching degree and I did my student teaching for fourth graders, we studied the moon phases. I taught it, but quite honestly most of what you'll hear today is directly from revelation I've been given from the Lord.

Brandon: Wow.

Julie: I think it's fascinating that this lunar eclipse and the alignment of the planets ties into my mission and the mission of the Gathering, as far as signs of the times.

The stars aligning tie into my mission specifically. My NDE was September 28th and 29th. The blood moon/lunar eclipse that happened in 2015 was on the 27th to the 28th of September, the anniversary for my 2004 NDE.

On that eleventh anniversary, I went into another near-death experience and I was sick in bed for about five days. During that time on the other side of the veil, they were teaching me that I was coming full circle. Just as this was the eleventh anniversary of my NDE, we were in the eleventh hour. We hear about that in the scriptures, don't we?

Brandon: Yeah, that's very significant.

Julie: So on my eleventh anniversary of my NDE, the Lord's messengers from the other side let me know that all would be well. I would be okay, and that particular sickness would not last much longer. I was given a priesthood blessing and some other healing to help me recover from that NDE. And I heard, "We are in the eleventh hour, Julie."

This is essentially just around the corner as we go into the twelfth hour, which signifies the return of the Savior. If you were to talk about a baseball game, we were in the bottom of the eighth inning, and that when we got to the bottom of the ninth inning we would be entering the tribulations. Entering the bottom of the ninth—the end of the baseball game, symbolically speaking—we would be entering the tribulations.

That ties into the stars and planets aligning. Anyone who wants to learn more about that can google and learn about Revelation 12 and the prophecies there that have been revealed for thousands of years. They are written in Revelation by John the Revelator, who is the same John that is in my book.

John the Revelator wrote about these planets aligning and he discussed this in Revelation 12. The beginning of the fulfillment of that prophecy will happen this September.

Brandon: Yeah. The crown of twelve stars. That's definitely a witness to me, and I can say that the Lord usually teaches us in ways that we can understand. Then when we recognize something one place and it reoccurs in other places, that's something to pay attention to.

Julie: Right. They've given me lessons on creation and other things. The first time I learned that was during my NDE. What they did is remind me of the lessons I had premortally, before I ever came to Earth. We've all had these science lessons, math lessons, and creation lessons, before we ever got a body and came to Earth.

When I had my NDE, they simply reminded me of what I had already been taught and of what was coming. When I was on the other side in spirit, then they showed me the past, present, and future.

So I have memories of other worlds, galaxies, and solar systems. I traveled to some of those places while I was in my NDE. I don't talk about those in the books, and this is the first time I am talking about it publicly, because people have a hard time believing that I would even travel on this earth or have experiences here.

So I usually try not to say much about that. But as we get closer to these planets aligning and the signs in the Heavens, I think it's important for people to know there will be a time-space overlap when we go into the Millennium. That's not exactly how it's gonna be, but that's the best human verbiage that I can come up to explain how time is kept in the eternities.

Brandon: We've heard it said that a thousand years on Earth is a day in God's time. In fact, time seems to be a construct of man, whereas God is not bound by time. That's hard to think about, because the only thing we know about God's time is "one eternal round."

There's obviously more to that. Science is now just discovering that there's more than ten dimensions. But anyway, before I get carried off track, basically you're saying there will be a time shift of sorts.

Julie: That's my understanding. Depending on the state in which you find yourself, whether that be angelic, translated, transfigured, resurrected, or a mortal being, time is kept differently. There's a lot that goes into it that we don't understand. I just have faith, because I've been able to experience some of that. So in theory I understand it, but in practice, I don't.

When I have dreams, I feel I am traveling intergalactically. I'm not staying on the Earth. So whether that's real or figurative, I don't know. That remains to be seen. But I have been able to see a lot through dreams and visions. I could describe to you in detail what the Great China Wall looks like, because I've been there so many times in dreams.

Brandon: That's amazing. I can actually relate to that as well. I think many people can who feel like they have dreams where they've been somewhere else.

Julie: I find it fascinating. I've had a lot of dreams about technology in the future being enhanced. I've been shown members of the City of Enoch coming back, and other people from other planets bringing cool aircraft. They come in some amazing aircraft that makes our technology right now look centuries old.

There are people on other planets who are more advanced in their technologies, and they're going to bring them to Earth. We were talking about the time-space overlap. That's the verbiage given to me to try to help people understand a little bit about what happens in different realms. What will happen in the Millennium is that I travel to many different places very quickly, so that I can do the Gathering work, missionary work, or whatever the Lord would have me do, serving a lot of different people for whatever His mission requires.

Brandon: You make me think of Visions of Glory, when Spencer describes his work. Once he reached New Jerusalem, he could literally be away on a mission for years and then he would return in what seemed like only a few minutes of time from when he began.

Julie: Right. My first real experience with this was when I was a child. I had visions from my earliest recollections. I just didn't know what to call them. I remember in fourth grade in Hawaii, being on the island of Oahu, and I would dream that I was going to the other islands.

Then I would have a lesson in my class, and the teacher would teach us about the islands. For instance, she'd tell us about the leper colony on one of the islands, and I had just dreamed I was there, visiting the lepers on that island. So from the time I was young, I've been trying to gain understanding as to how some of this works.

Then when I had my NDE in 2004, I was in the emergency room and in a bad state of mind. I was lucid, but I had the Epstein Barr virus attack my body. We later discovered I also have Lyme disease, but the Epstein Barr virus is what actually put me into the state that I was in.

I felt I was in the emergency room for about ten minutes, but when I got out of the hospital I asked my husband, and he said we were there for nearly seven hours. Time flew so quickly because my spirit was essentially detaching from my body and I was seeing things on the other side of the veil. It flew by so quickly. For everybody else who was there, it felt like an eternity, right?

But for me, I was in a very happy state. I was surrounded by loved ones on the other side of the veil and having visionary experiences. I was having a wonderful time and I was so calm, even though I was sick. My spirit was very happy because of who was attending me. My grandma and grandpa, and some other people on the other side of the veil.

That was one of the of the most pronounced experiences I had before my NDE. That was the day that I went into the hospital the first time, and that night I left my body and experienced what I described in my book *A Greater Tomorrow*.

Some people will say: "Oh, she's crazy. That was just her being in a psychosis." I can testify that's not what it was. The illness was causing my spirit to detach.

Your spirit body and your physical body can detach when you're in enough pain, whether that be physical, mental, spiritual, or emotional. My body was so sick that it just slipped out of my body, if you will, but it wasn't entirely out of my body. I think that's fascinating, right?

Brandon: I can actually relate to that myself, even on relatively minor things, like food poisoning or dehydration. There were times when I remember getting strong impressions and a sense of alarm, not because of the pain or what I was going through, but a new feeling of anxiety. I felt I could pass out, or somehow not be around anymore. I didn't think that it meant death, but it did feel like my spirit would slip away. That's the best way to describe that.

Julie: Like an out-of-body experience.

Brandon: Yeah, based on what you were talking about with your NDEs and the conditions you were suffering through. I think the world greatly misunderstands what people go through as far as even something as simple as a coma.

I think there's a great deal of misunderstanding. Our lives here are also purpose built. There's a very specific goal to receive the experience we need,and to choose between good and evil, and thereby return to His presence.

It's so personal. We don't have the words to describe simple things that we experience in this life, let alone somebody that was born with a very severe mental illness and was never able to speak.

Julie: I appreciate that Brandon. That leads me into my health issues, because I don't have anything to hide. The adversary has tried to make me afraid to tell my story, and he's really tried to invoke fear upon me since 2004. He has sent lots of his messengers to haunt me and to badger me, trying to tell me that if I were to go public with my story, people would just think I'm crazy, and even go so far as to lock me up.

What that did, initially, was invoke fear in me. Then as I've worked through that, I've realized it's motivated me to share more of my story and to let people know that I don't have anything to hide.

There is so much more that comes into play with mental illness or any other physical, mental or emotional affect on the body. In my book I talk about how hard it was for me to come back to earth. One of the biggest reasons was because they explained what my health issues were gonna be. They told me that I was gonna come back with mental illness, and I sobbed and sobbed.

I have memories of putting my hands in my face, sitting in a room after I was shown the Window of Heaven. Then they gave me some time to myself, and I just sobbed because I didn't want to cause pain to anyone else, and I didn't want to have to go through the pain. Even though I understood that I had agreed to it, I did not want to face the pain and anguish I was gonna go through.

I have dealt with a lot of physical pain, but I can tell you that mental illness is more painful to me than some of the worst physical pain I've been through. Then to come back to a body that I knew was going to be very sick was almost more than I could bear. What were people gonna say about me? Plus, I knew it was gonna be at least nine years before I would get to tell my story, and not even having my husband or other people close to me believe me. I knew I would come back and not have a single soul that I could talk to about this for a long time.

That in and of itself was painful on the other side of the veil, but then they reminded me of what I committed to premortally. They reminded me of the benefits that would come in going through that. They promised me amazing blessings in my life, and one of those amazing blessings was to be able to convert souls to Christ. They reminded me of my love for the Savior.

Brandon: Yeah.

Julie: (crying) I remembered how much I wanted to be with Him, and how much I love my Father in Heaven. I resolved that I was gonna just get it together, and I would come back to my body on Earth and do what I had committed to do premortally. I would do what I knew was right, which was to warn and testify and to tell people how much I love the Lord. I committed to do whatever I needed to do to bring as many people home because this is the time of The Gathering.

That is why I do this, Brandon. I know it wasn't a figment of my imagination, and what has happened to me since waking up regarding all of the adversarial attacks and all of the opposition, and also all of the blessings and the tremendous spiritual intervention that has occurred to keep me alive and to heal my body. There are no words for that.

The more I go along in this process and the closer we get to the tribulations starting, the more convinced I am that I absolutely made the right choice. No price is too great to pay to return to Father in Heaven and to return to the Savior. If can be successful in that and help others to be successful, then I consider my job well done.

I know the promises He's given me are gonna come to fruition. One of the things I was promised was complete healing one day, no matter how much pain and anguish I would endure. I would have an entirely new body, whole and complete, without pain. Then when that part of my mission is over, I get to travel the world to do missionary work, and that is what brings me joy.

Brandon: I can definitely add my name to the list of souls that you've brought closer to Christ. I know that through hearing your testimony, I have absolutely felt so much closer to the Savior. I have felt Him in ways that I'd always suspected, but had never realized until that time. So I just wanted to thank you for that as well.

Julie: Thank you, Brandon. I appreciate your friendship, I appreciate the work you do with our organization, and I appreciate your testimony, your witness, and your questions today. I think we'll wrap it up here. I just want to turn it over to Eric and see if he has anything he wants to add.

Eric: Well, it's been really fun to be a fly on the wall in this conversation. I'm pretty content where I am. I've had a number of thoughts but I think we can let those go until another podcast.

Julie: Okay. Well, I just appreciate both of you. I'm thankful for your friendship, for your strengths, your witness and your testimonies, and I look forward to doing another podcast with both of you.

PODCAST 3

⸙

SPIRITUAL GIFTS

Julie: We'd like to welcome you to the Julie Rowe Show today. We've got another great podcast lined up, and I've got Eric Smith on the line. Eric, how are you today?

Eric: Doing great.

Julie: Great! Today I'll be answering questions that Eric has. He's got some great ideas, so I'll turn the time over to him.

Eric: Sounds good. Julie, on the first podcast we talked about the Wasatch Wakeup. Toward the end we started talking about some visionary insights that you had as a girl, and got me thinking, "Well, that would be an interesting podcast."

While writing your biography, I've heard a lot of interesting stories of your gifts, beginning with when you were a child. I'd like to broaden that to the topic of spiritual gifts. The doctrinal premise for this topic comes from First Corinthians chapter 12. It feels to me almost like a forgotten chapter, or a forgotten doctrine, even in Christianity.

Paul talks about the gifts of healing the gifts of tongues, speaking in tongues, interpretation of tongues, and so forth. He mentions the gift of prophesying.

One of my early thoughts after I read your books was, "You know, I really believe this woman's story is legitimate." But I always had cultural doubts in the back of my mind, for example, "Wait. This is a woman. Can women prophesy?" or "Shouldn't visionary experiences be restricted to select groups of people?"

Call them leaders, call them highly spiritual people, whatever you want, and I had to battle with those thoughts. I've come to conclude on my own, with the assistance of the Holy Ghost, that spiritual gifts are real and that they can be exercised and practiced by anyone. I just wanted to hear your thoughts on that and maybe delve into your childhood as much as you want. Tell any stories you have had with your gifts.

Julie: Wow! Okay! That's great, Eric. I think this is gonna be a fascinating topic to discuss today. I also have had a lot of time to think about this topic. Obviously in respect to my own life, in trying to understand who I am, where I come from, and why I'm here, I've had some of those deeper questions I think every individual asks at some point in their life. They're trying to understand their origin, why they're on this planet, and why they have certain gifts.

We all have them. We've all been endowed and created in the image of our Father and given certain gifts from the beginning before we came to this earth. We brought them with us. It says in the Scriptures that we all have been granted from the Father at least one spiritual gift, the Light of Christ.

They come with that spiritual gift, and in many cases they come with several gifts. I'm not gonna take time on this podcast to try to explain some of my understanding as to why one person may have one gift and not another, or how come some people seem to have a lot of spiritual gifts that are more evident to the eye and other people seem to be lacking.

I have been taught by the Spirit on some of that, where we come from, how old we are, spiritually speaking, and where we lived before we came. But I'm keeping it as simple as I can today by talking about some of the simple experiences I had as a child, and into my young adult years. So thank you for asking that Eric. As you've mentioned, you and I have spent quite a lot of time talking over the telephone and done some in-person interviews to write my biography. How many recordings do think we've done, Eric?

Eric: Hard to say. I would guess in the area of 200 hours, probably.

Julie: Right. A fair amount. So you've gotten to know me pretty well over the phone, and I have shared a lot with you that I haven't shared with other people.

I have shared things with Eric in a recording situation where I have been able to open up with him, and he knows I'm not making this stuff up. I have been able to consistently talk to him about some of the experiences that I've had that relate to spiritual gifts.

At this point in time, I don't entirely understand it either. I don't necessarily always know why I experience them or why someone does or doesn't experience them. I'm doing the best with those that the Lord has given me. I have a long way to go in trying to understand what they are and how I should best utilize them to serve the Lord.

I remember some things happening to me very early on, in my early toddler years. One of them that I will talk about is one I have discussed with Eric. I was living in Texas and a bird landed on my head.

What do you remember about that, Eric? Why don't you tell the story the best you remember it. I'm curious to know what your interpretation was.

Eric: All right, my recollection is you were in the backyard, you were maybe seven or eight, or something.

Julie: I was three.

Eric: (laughing) Okay, a little off there.

Julie: (laughing) That's okay! I was three years old, in the backyard, playing on the swing set.

Eric: Your sister needed to run inside, and as she was running inside, you had the sensation of a bird up in the tree. You saw beforehand that the bird would come down, land on your head, and perch there for a minute. Your mom was watching from the back and everybody was just fascinated by this bird on your head. You were just so curious, maybe a little afraid at first at why this bird was on you.

So first of all, it was significant to me that you sensed it would happen. Then secondly, I remember you having a little bit of communication with the bird. Just a very simple communication that things were okay and that the bird liked you.

Julie: That's great. You got it right! The only thing you didn't get was my age. That's pretty good!

Eric: (laughing) Yeah.

Julie: So yes, I was three years old, on the swing set. My sister went in to use the restroom, and as she did my mom opened the back door. As Eric mentioned, I both sensed and saw in advance that the bird was gonna land on me.

I heard a voice from the other side of the veil say to me, "The bird's gonna land on your head, but don't be afraid." Then that bird flew down, landed on my head just like I had foreseen, and sat there for a good two or three minutes.

I don't know how often that happens, but I think it's quite remarkable that a bird would sit on a three-year-old girl's head. I remember asking that voice, "Why is the bird on my head?" The simple answer was essentially, "It's okay, it just likes you."

I was afraid and cried out to my mom, "What do I do? What do I do?! The bird's on my head!"

She said, "It's okay. Let it stay there, it'll fly away in a minute." But it didn't. It just stayed. After a couple of minutes of that, I had a little bit of silent conversation with the bird. There was an understanding that the bird just liked me, and it just wanted to sit there for a minute.

At that time, I had these images of Disney princesses in my head. I was trying to make sense through the view of a three-year-old girl who watched movies like Snow White.

"Am I like Snow White?" I thought. "Do I have magical powers like Snow White? She can talk to animals."

It was very real in my mind, and being assisted by those on the other side of the veil, it solidified that there was something of a spiritual nature to this event, and that I wasn't making it up.

At that age, the veil was very thin for me, and I was having visits from people from the other side. That was all I knew. I didn't know anything differently. I came into this world with those gifts and that was my life. I didn't understand that not everyone experienced that.

Eric: Did you talk to other people about those gifts?

Julie: Not like that. I remember talking to my mom about the bird and asking her why it landed on my head. She said, "I think the bird just thought your hair was it's nest."

Because I have dark brown hair, and I saw that most birds build nests out of dark brown materials, that seemed like a pretty good logical answer to tell a three-year-old. But in my heart I knew I'd had a silent communication with the bird. It was somehow directed by the Spirit to do that as a teaching lesson for me.

Eric: I find that really sweet. I was wondering if you could jump up in age and talk about some of your experiences with natural disasters or calamities, and your gifts in relation to those.

Julie: We soon moved to Washington state, where I was in kindergarten through the first part of third grade. I had quite a few spiritual experiences while living there.

One time I went next door to my neighbor's house. They invited me to come to their backyard. They had older children, and their daughter had grown up. She had left her dolls and her little rocking chair and other furniture for her dolls. They didn't get much use, so our neighbors invited me to come play in their backyard to play with their daughter's dolls.

While I was sitting there playing with these dolls, I had a person from the other side of the veil come visit me. She was a beautiful woman. I never told anyone that. To this day my family actually doesn't know that. I told my mom once, several years ago. I don't know if she'd remember.

At first it was a little bit of a scary situation because I wasn't expecting a visitor. Then it was very endearing and special for me, because it was my great-grandmother from the other side of the veil that came to minister to me.

She told me a few things. She said I was a very special girl, and that Heavenly Father had given me some special gifts. I shouldn't be afraid of them, and that I should use those gifts to love my brothers and sisters in my family and in the world.

She said that as long as I was a good little girl, and I did everything that Heavenly Father asked me to do, He would continue to bestow other gifts on me that I could use to show love to Heavenly Father's children.

Eric: Interesting. I haven't heard that story, so it's nice to know you've still got a few up your sleeve. What I find interesting is that you didn't tell anyone about that experience. Why didn't you talk about those things with other people?

Julie: Well, I came from a large family and we moved around a lot. My parents were deeply spiritual people, but they were very busy people and I was a shy child, initially. I had to overcome my shyness. Also, I lived in a household where although we talked about spiritual things, we did not talk about dreams and visions or things like that. I had no context for it at that age, and no one in my extended family lived near us. I didn't have grandparents near us, and I didn't have aunts and uncles or cousins that we grew up with.

I was very close to my siblings, but I was the second oldest of ten kids, so they were all younger. I would sometimes try to talk to my older sister, and she was a great friend to me, but I didn't ever feel safe sharing those kinds of things.

I emotionally withheld them. There were times when I would pray to Heavenly Father and ask Him specifically, "Can I tell anyone? Can I tell my sister?"

I think that's pretty amazing too, that at the age of seven, eight, and nine, somehow I knew I could ask Heavenly Father for permission to share things, and I could hear from the Spirit, "No honey, it's better if you just keep this to yourself."

Eric: Hmm. Interesting.

Julie: So I actually would pray about it, and I followed that pattern all through my life where I would ask Heavenly Father, "Can I tell so and so? Can I tell this to my Bishop? Can I tell this to my Dad or my Mom? Can I tell this to my boyfriend? Can I tell this to my best friend?"

I would continually ask, and in most cases I was told it wasn't something that was wise to do. That was for my protection, although I didn't know that word at the time. They would just say, "It's better that you don't."

Then combine that with the adversary just heaping on me. There were constantly those from the other side that were not of the Light, sending me fear messages from a very early age, telling me if I told someone, they would think I was crazy.

I started hearing those messages through thought, starting with that experience with the bird. That was my first profound experience with somebody from the other side of the veil that was of the Light. Then the adversary stepped in right away and said, "You can't tell anyone what really happened here, because they're gonna think you're crazy. They're gonna think you're a bad little girl. They're gonna think that you have bad magic powers."

There were a lot of things that the adversary did from a very young age and it just increased. Especially after I was baptized into the LDS Church at the age of eight. It was remarkably more difficult after I got baptized of how the adversary worked on me.

That fear energy kind of took hold for a while. When I did feel like I wanted to share an experience with someone, the adversary was right there telling me, "You can't do that, because they won't like you anymore." As a little girl in third and fourth grade, we wanna be liked. We don't wanna be different. Even though I knew I was different than a lot of my friends, I didn't want them to know how different I was, even in my family.

So I would ask questions. I would say to my friends, "Does this ever happen to you?"

I would test the waters and I would ask my Dad or my Mom, or I would ask my brothers and sisters, especially my older sister. I would ask her: "Has this ever happened to you?"

I wouldn't get a positive answer. I never found anybody who could agree with me or who could relate to an experience like that. So when you're testing the waters like that and no one comes back and says, "Yeah, that happens to me," why would I tell anyone?

Eric: You were an astute young girl to be that intuitive and to understand how to read people's body language and read the cues in their verbal expressions. I find that really interesting.

Julie: I did have a natural gift for it very early on, and it is a blessing. Sometimes it felt like a curse because I was able to often read their energy and body language, and even read their thoughts in some cases. Not the exact thought, but the thought energy would come at me and I would understand the basic energy coming out of their minds or their hearts.

That caused a lot of pain, too, because sometimes people would think things about me or someone else, not knowing that I could pick up on that. I trapped a lot of emotions that way.

Eric: Interesting. Okay, can you tell us any experiences with natural occurrences or nature?

Julie: Yeah. So getting back to your original question. One big one was in Hawaii. I got to take a trip to the Big Island of Hawaii for my fourth grade class. While there, we walked near the Kilauea Crater.

I was shown in dream and vision before I went on that trip because it came in the second semester, and all school year we were looking forward to this trip. I started dreaming about that trip probably six months in advance, and I would dream about it almost every night.

I would dream about different things we were gonna do on the Island, and what we were gonna learn. We were studying the Hawaiian language and culture, including learning about things that had happened of a spiritual sense on the Islands. We learned about Captain Cook and what happened with the white people settling the islands and things like that.

We were also studying volcanoes, and one of our projects was to do a topographical, three-dimensional map and then make a volcano. My group was assigned the Big Island of Hawaii, and we had to do the Kilauea Volcano three-dimensionally out of paper mache' prior to our trip.

While we were working on that I would have visionary experiences. I had several dreams and day visions that the Kilauea Volcano was going to erupt while we were on the Big Island. I thought it'd be really cool, but I was kind of afraid of it.

I even told my teacher, who I just loved and adored, of my anxiety related to Kilauea Volcano and what I was seeing. I never told her why. I just said I was afraid that the volcano was gonna erupt while we were on the Big Island.

I asked specific questions like, "How far is our camp from the crater of the volcano?" and "How long would it take for the volcano, if it was gonna erupt, to reach our camp?"

I saw in vision that it was gonna erupt, and I was afraid that was gonna come to pass. We walked to the crater the day before Kilauea Volcano erupted for the first time in a hundred years. It erupted while I was at the KOA that no longer exists, because it has erupted so many times that it destroyed the KOA.

As we walked near the crater, the geologists were there intensely studying the Kilauea Volcano, because they knew it could blow any day. They weren't sure if they were gonna let our group go up to the lookout points, due to the risk involved. We had to wait outside when we got to that place.

When we got up to the lookout points, they went ahead and let us do it because they decided that it would be fine for another day or so. They said it could blow the next day, or in a week, or in a month. Honestly, from everything they were studying, it was pretty risky to let us up there.

We got to look through the viewing glasses at the look-out point, then we left. Then the next evening before sunset I got to see in the distance Kilauea Volcano erupting for the first time in a hundred years. Then our evening plans got cancelled because of the volcano, so we got to go outside and watch the eruption. I don't know how many miles away it was from KOA, but it was close enough that we could see it in the distance. At that time, there wasn't any potential harm for us.

Eric: Interesting.

Julie: Then that night as it was erupting, I had dreams that the lava was going to reach the KOA and destroy it. It caused me great anxiety, because I was afraid that it would get to us before we could get out. I didn't have a context for time on that, because I'd already dreamed that it was gonna erupt and it happened the very next day.

As a little kid, not ever being around a volcano like that before,

I didn't know and I couldn't judge distance. I really don't know how long it took. It might've taken a year or two before it even reached the KOA. I just know it doesn't exist now.

But I remember asking my school teacher, "Can the lava get to us? Because we're gonna be here for another four days and I'm kinda worried that the lava's gonna get too close to us."

Eric: So you'll see things that may not happen with you nearby, or even while you're there, but it may happen at some point in the future.

Julie: Right. I don't always have context for it, because it's often as if I'm there when I see it, in a real-time vision or a night vision. There are different types of day visions that people experience. You can see it opened up in front of you, as if you're really watching it, or you can have one in your mind's eye. There are a lot of different ways that people have visions, and I've experienced all of those in one form or another.

Eric: I really appreciate hearing that because as I read the Scriptures, I tend to read about one type of experience, a visionary experience. You're helping me understand that there are all kinds of degrees of revelation and revelatory experiences.

Julie: Right. You can have a deja vu experience, you can have a dream, you can have a night vision, and you can have a live vision where the veil opens up and you see everything in real time like it's going on right now. There are a lot of different ways that you have visionary experiences and gifts.

Eric: You've mentioned in the past some things about Mount Rainier and Mount St. Helens. Do you have anything to go with that?

Julie: I'm glad you're bringing this up, because it's so hard to write about it and it's hard to speak on it. I kind of skipped over that when I was talking earlier about Washington state, so thank you.

During my time there, a couple of significant things happened, one of which was the Mount St. Helens eruption. That was huge. Similar to the Kilauea Volcano experience, I saw in vision several months in advance that Mount St. Helens was going to erupt.

I think we had four to six kids in the family during that time. My parents tried to keep their young children active on a Sabbath Day, because we were not allowed to play outside or to play with our friends on Sunday. That was one of our family rules. So my parents would take us on Sunday drives.

We would go on a Sunday drive for an hour and a half, maybe two hours at the most. We would go onto the two-lane highways. I remember the tall pine trees on both sides of the road, and driving and driving.

As a little kid, when you drive for an hour in the car with your parents with nothing but nature to see, it kind of seems like a long time. We would look in the distance, and my dad would point out Mount St. Helens every time, and Mount Rainier.

Since I had seen both of those in vision, erupting, I remember asking my dad, "Am I gonna be on this road when it blows up? What happens if it blows and I'm just in my car with my family? Am I gonna die?"

Then I remember the Spirit calming me down. I learned a lot about how the Spirit works as a young child through these experiences, because the Spirit would come in and calm my heart. The Holy Ghost would tell me that I was safe, and that I didn't need to worry. I was told to just be a good girl and listen to my mom and dad, and no harm would come to me.

After seeing Mount St. Helens in vision erupting, then actually having it happen was quite surreal. I was in my house and I watched the ash fall. I watched people go crazy while they collected it in jars and cups, and all kinds of stuff.

The ash went all the way over to Yakima. We had good friends that lived there, and when we visited them they showed us how much ash had dropped on them. It affected Puget Sound and other things. It was all over the news. It was a big deal.

Eric: As you're seeing this unfold on the news and you're seeing the ash, did you know instantly that your vision had come true?

Julie: I did. It was so surreal and yet so unreal. Nothing had ever happened like that in my lifetime, or anyone else's. Everybody else was making a big deal about it. Schools were shut down, churches were shut down, stores were shut down.

It was the first time in my life that I saw a natural disaster, close to home, that affected drinking water, groceries on the shelves, and people's safety. I heard stories about people who didn't evacuate, and they died. I heard all that, and my parents watched it on the news.

That is the first time in my young heart that I decided, "When I grow up, I'm gonna make sure I have food at my house, and I have water to drink, so if I ever have a earthquake or if I ever have a volcano…"

I was just trying to minimize my anxiety at a very young age. Then later on, we moved to Hawaii and lived through a hurricane. My parents weren't super fanatical about food storage, but they always tried to have some. Even in the military, we would get rid of furniture, we'd get rid of toys, we'd get rid of a lot of things that I would have liked to have kept as a young child, but my parents would keep the flour and the sugar.

Eric: (laughing) The important stuff, yeah.

Julie: Right. That left a strong impression on me as a young child.

Eric: Well, the biography will cover a number of other sweet little stories where Julie had visionary experiences and dreams. I think your listeners and readers will find those really enjoyable and really endearing. They'll find another side to Julie Rowe that they just don't know.

Julie: Thank you, Eric.

Eric: Now let's bring it home. Obviously your gifts have continued on to our current days. You've seen things that will happen in the future, and anyone who hasn't read your books could read those to find out what those things are.

I guess I wanna drive it home to the viewers. Do you believe that spiritual gifts are accessible and attainable to the common man, for lack of a better phrase?

Julie: I believe they're attainable for everyone. We are all created in God's image, and you are on the path to be like Him. Having been created like our Heavenly Parents, we have the potential to have every single gift that God has. He will bestow that upon us when we're ready for it, according to our individual plan. He has a Plan of Happiness created specifically for us.

So what's right for one isn't necessarily right for another. I believe that we are entering into a new dispensation where we are going to see spiritual gifts come alive like we have never seen before. That is gonna be a beautiful thing as we start gathering the Lord's people together and watching as these spiritual gifts awaken in people. They will come to realize their divine potential.

Eric: That's terrific. That's really encouraging. I wanna just add my witness that in the time that I've followed your story, read your books, and listened to your radio shows, that I really took it seriously. I took my questions to the Lord, and I really wanted to know if you were allowed to see the things that you had seen.

I found that within a short time, my own gifts began to bolster and I began having dreams and visions. I actually realized that I'd had some significant dreams and visions before I really got serious about these questions. I just consider myself a regular, common person, and I just wanna add my witness that spiritual gifts are real. I feel like we live in a day where they're swept under the rug, and people think that you're crazy, because it's so unusual. Do you have anything to say about the culture and the current circumstances of spiritual gifts and the way that society views them?

Julie: I think that's a reflection on the darkness that's on this earth right now in trying to sweep spiritual gifts under the rug. Everyone has these gifts, whether they realize that or not. The dark side uses their powers to try to dissuade people from knowing who their true identity is and who they really are. They try to keep us from understanding our divine potential.

So absolutely they are being swept away. Not because people don't have them, but because people are not acknowledging them. They're not recognizing the Source of where those gifts come from. Every single gift that we have is from God.

I consider it a spiritual gift if a man is able to work hard. I think it's a spiritual gift to be able to have faith, or to be able to teach your children. I think it's a spiritual gift to be able to do anything in this world, because we are all created in His image. Everything we have, we owe to the Lord. Everything we do, we owe to the Lord. Everything we are is because of Him. They are all gifts given to us from the Lord.

Eric: That's great. So I gather from that comment that you don't think you're more special than other people, because of your gifts?

Julie: I know I'm not. I know that the Lord has given these gifts to me for a specific purpose to fulfil His plan in my life, and in whatever lives I can influence for good. It's not because I'm any better than anyone. The Lord has given me these gifts because He's trusting that I will do with them what He's asked me to do.

Eric: I agree with that. I have one last thought. As you were talking, I was kind of sympathizing with those in the world who know they have gifts but who hunker down. They close it in, they don't tell people, and I just feel sympathy for them. Do you have anything in your mind or your heart about people in that situation?

Julie: I do. I appreciate that because I empathize greatly with each person who feels that way, having been through that myself. I'm still struggling to overcome that, like a caged bird, or having my wings clipped.

It's time that we rise above that. I see a new generation coming, and I see a new uprising for Light. We will gather together in truth and in harmony, uniting for the Lord's purposes to combat evil on this planet.

As we do that, we take stewardship and ownership of who we are, the Lord's children. We are the very elect who will gather together and combat the forces of evil, prior to the Second Coming and going into the Millennium.

I promise you that as you take ownership of your gifts, and as you rise above the adversary and you shake off the shackles, those gifts will increase exponentially. You will find greater strength and power in the Priesthood of God, and you will be able to tackle whatever comes to you. I say that in Christ's name, because that is Who is behind this mission. That is Who is behind this cause. That is Who is behind The Gathering. He promised me, and He promises you that as well.

Eric: Thanks Julie, that's a powerful witness. Thanks for taking the time to answer these questions that are really dear to my heart. I also thank you for being such a good example of someone who holds their gifts in humility, and is using them for blessing other people.

Julie: Well, I live every day struggling like the rest of us, Eric. Anybody who knows me knows how imperfect I am. But

I appreciate your encouragement as I try to do whatever it is the Lord wants me to do. I'm thankful for everybody that's doing their part. I love you guys.

PODCAST 4

—✣—

OVERPOWERING EVIL

Julie: We'd like to welcome you to the Julie Rowe Show today. We've got a great podcast lined up, and we've got Eric Smith on the line. Hi Eric!

Eric: Hi there, Julie.

Julie: Today we thought we would talk about some of the issues that inflict us here on Planet Earth. Expressly the topic of demons, devils, disembodied or unclean spirits.

Then the counter to that, guardian and ministering angels, who helps us heal and minister to us. This is a topic of interest. I've had thousands of people email me, and several hundred of them ask questions about how to handle some of these experiences they're having in their lives.

So after talking to Eric about what we could do a podcast on, we decided together that this would be a good way to do a basic overview or introduction for those who are seeking a little bit more information. Maybe they have need for a little bit of clarity. There's a lot of fear energy revolving around things like ghosts, demons, and devils.

We will try to dispel some of that energy, and also spread truth about the importance of knowing the Light from the dark and being able to discern spirits, like we are hearing from our leaders and from those in the Scriptures. As we move forward into the future tribulations, it's extremely important that we learn how to deal with these entities and unclean spirits. We also need to learn how to invite Light into our lives so that we can have added power.

I'm gonna turn the question time over to Eric and see what he has for me. None of these are pre-planned. We just come up with a topic and start talking. So let's see where this goes, Eric.

Eric: Sure. As I've been thinking about the topic, some things have come to my mind. I'm gonna start there, and you can respond as you see fit.

I was seventeen years old when I first read through the New Testament and had a change of heart. I knew that Jesus Christ was the son of God and that He was the Savior of the World. More personally, I knew that He was my Savior, and I felt darkness leave my life. I was grateful for Him.

I also saw early on that Jesus spent an awful lot of His mortal mission casting out devils. I mean, He gave fine sermons and He healed the sick, but my goodness, He spent a lot of His time casting out devils, demons, unclean spirits, and rebuking them.

It makes me think about where we are today. I feel like we live in a pretty evil world and yet, there's hardly any mention of the devil. Those who do mention the devil tend to be considered or viewed as a little crazy, maybe even a little old-fashioned. I just find it interesting that it was such a focus for Him in His day, but it's not focused on or talked about hardly at all in our day.

Julie: I find that interesting as well. I can personally attest to the fact that people do think you're a little bit strange in our society if you talk about the Spirit Realm. I've had a lot of negative energy come at me, a lot of emails, and people come up to me at speaking events calling me names and sending other negative energy.

I believe at the root of that is fear energy. It's completely inspired by the adversary because he does not want people to be exposed to

Truth and Light of any sort. He especially does not want them to have power to combat the evil forces that are at war against us here on the Earth.

I find it interesting, too, that it's expressly in the Scriptures, time and time again. We have the pattern there. We don't have a lot of instruction of how He actually did it, but there are places where we can learn of these things. I think it's extremely important in our daily lives, but it's even more important going into the tribulations.

It is going to be increasingly important for us to be able to know how to cast out these unclean disembodied spirits, or invite them to go to the Light. That's the first line that I see. I feel like most of the unclean spirits are confused, more than anything else.

Then we have the entities which are the actual devils and demons that have been part of the one-third that were cast out in the premortal realm before we came to Earth.

Of course, we've got people in the Christian faiths that don't even believe that we had a world before we came to this world. I testify to you that I know I lived somewhere before I came to Planet Earth. I have several memories of it, and they're not false memories.

When I had my NDE's, I was shown those are correct memories and experiences. So we first have to come to an understanding of our true nature and our Divine Nature, and our Divine Origin, which is: Earth is not our original home.

We came from a Spirit Home, a Spirit Realm before we ever came here. We were created in Spirit before we ever had a physical body. When people realize that, it opens up their hearts and their minds to the other possibilities that exist.

For instance, there really was a War in Heaven where a third of the Hosts of Heaven were cast out with Satan when he rebelled against God and tried to take God's Glory upon himself. But one of the deceptions of the adversary is to try to convince people to not believe that there even is a devil.

Eric: It's sort of an ironic thing that he would try to get us not to believe in him. I was on a website a while back, looking through comments and somebody mentioned, "This person's deceived by the devil" or something, and then somebody came back with a follow-up comment that said, "The devil, ha ha, there's no such thing. Whoever invented the devil with horns, their only purpose was to invoke fear in people. There's no such thing as the devil."

I thought to myself, "This person has taken the information straight from the devil and bought it hook, line, and sinker."

Julie: Right. Well, one of the lines the adversary uses is, "There's no such thing as the devil. You don't even need to be afraid of me."

If you are on the Earth today, you have a body and you chose God's Plan. You did choose to follow Christ, at least enough to get a body and come to Earth, and, you did vote in favor of God's Plan that was foreordained and pre-planned before the Earth was even created.

So those that come to Earth and have bodies, first need to acknowledge that there is a God. We have a Father in Heaven who loves us, who had a plan for us, who created this Earth and that He has a Son. I testify to you that they are two separate Beings. When I had my Near Death Experience, I saw both of them. I do not talk about that in my book, due to the personal and sacred nature of my relationship with them and what I experienced.

I will now stand boldly in letting you know that I know, one hundred percent, without a doubt, we have both a Father in Heaven and a Brother, His Son Jesus Christ, and also the Holy Spirit, who is another Personage of Spirit. All three make up the Godhead in unity, working One in Purpose.

But there are some false doctrines that have been taught since the beginning of man, when Cain slew Abel. That was one of the points in history when some of those lies and deceptions started here on the Earth. They started premortally, though.

I remember some specific things and the Spirit has continued to remind me that in the War in Heaven, Satan was extremely crafty. He was actually quite handsome and charming, and he was extremely knowledgeable in the Powers and Priesthoods of our Father. One of his biggest lines was, "You don't need to follow God, you don't need to follow Christ. Follow me. You don't want to rely on Christ for the Atonement, because you might not make it back home. But if you choose my plan, I can guarantee you safety. I can guarantee that you're gonna be able to do whatever you want, you're gonna have power, and I can teach you everything I know."

That was just one of the lines that he gave. He invoked fear in people, even then. He said if they chose his plan, he could "guarantee recovery" or "guarantee that they could go home."

That is a lie. He still does it every day, in different methods. That is one of the reasons I wanna do this podcast, because I am so tired of the lies and the deceptions that have been going on that we see in hundredfold today.

They are everywhere in our society. They are masked, they are cloaked, yet they are now being so blunt with their affronts that they've infiltrated everything! They're in our media, they're in our children's toys, they're in our school systems, they're in our churches, and they're in our congregations. I mean, everything! The false traditions and false lies are absolutely nauseating to me.

Eric: You mentioned bodies a minute ago. Many of the children of Father chose to come to Earth and get a body, and those who didn't, did not receive a body. So that presents an interesting situation where those who didn't get bodies, now want bodies, and so they possess them.

When we hear about possession, I think a lot of us think about foaming at the mouth, gnashing the teeth, and convulsing and shaking on the ground. Do you see it like that?

Julie: I have seen situations where people behave like that, but 99 percent of the time that is not what it looks like when someone has been possessed. Often people have a possession or a spirit attachment, which is a little bit different, and the spirit attachment can be from disembodied spirits as well. That often occurs, and people don't even know that it's occurring, because that spirit has been attached to them or has been in possession for so long, they think it's part of who they are.

That can happen for a variety of reasons, and sometimes very early on in age. That is one of the many explanations for why we have a lot of the health issues we do. It's not the only reason, but it is sometimes a huge factor.

That's also one of the other reasons I see a lot of other ills that we have in society. That's a topic that makes people upset, fearful, and angry because they don't feel like they have any control over what's going on with their body. They think that dark energy can come in and around and through people, and that there's nothing we can do about it. But there is something we can do about it, and that is what this podcast is about. We're gonna help some people with that today.

Eric: So do you think people are possessed all around us?

Julie: Every day, all around me, I see people possessed. With some of the spiritual gifts that I have, I can often discern spirit attachments or spirit possessions. It doesn't just come from entities.

I want to make it clear that the entities are men that were cast out in the war in heaven, and the disembodied or unclean spirits are men *and* women who were born and died on this earth, and still linger here.

The War in Heaven is real. It's gone on for centuries. Since the fall of Adam we have had devils upon the earth. Even the false traditions regarding Mother Eve and Father Adam are absolutely an affront to the Spirit. The Lord planned for The Fall and gave us the opportunity to be on the Earth to be tempted and tried by those same adversarial spirits. Through these experiences we can grow and learn how to become like Him. How else do we learn to be victorious in spiritual warfare, other than to just go through it?

Eric: Right. You mentioned ways of getting the devil out of you. How do we first recognize that maybe we have devils or unclean spirits clinging to us, or even within us?

Julie: That's a hard question, Eric, because not everyone has the same spiritual gifts. Most people can't see them, right? They are veiled, which is part of the plan here on earth.

I need to make it very clear that the veil is a blessing to us. It can often feel frustrating not to be able to see things. I've had a lot of people who have said, "You're so lucky that you had an NDE" or "You're so lucky that you have such gifts."

Be assured that it comes at a cost. It comes at a cost of accountability. If you're gonna see the light, then there is the opposite in all things, so you see the dark. I see the whole spectrum. There have been times when I have been in the darkest abyss that people cannot imagine.

There are very dark worlds and dark dimensions that people do not even realize exist. I think it's a tender mercy of the Lord that He veiled our eyes while we're in a Telestial state so that we're not subjected to that knowledge and therefore held accountable. I have had attacks placed upon me, in part, because they know that I have seen the Light, and they know the claims that I have made. Because of that, if I'm gonna claim that I've seen God, then it stands to reason I've seen Satan. He is a nasty dude, and you don't want to have a face to face with him just for fun.

There are people that get involved in some of that stuff. I do not know why anybody would ever want to get involved in any of that dark energy. There are people on the planet that willfully engage in dark arts and other things, and it's entrapment.

There are so many different ways that the adversary comes to people. He'll come and tell them he can teach them things, he'll tell them he has shortcuts, he'll tell them that they don't need God, that they can just use him, he can teach them powers and priesthoods. There's so many different reasons why Satan does what he does, but the ultimate goal he has is to control and destroy.

He seeks to have dominion, not only of the earth but of a lot of other places. He is seeking to be able to accelerate in his dark powers. There are places that are unspeakably dark that I would not wish upon my worst enemy. My heart goes out to those who are trapped in those dark places.

I have hope that those who are unclean spirits, and I'll clarify, that disembodied unclean spirits are those who have lived on the earth and have had bodies, both men and women.

There are a variety of reasons as to why someone would be on this Earth in the Spirit Realm and not move on to the Light. They often have addictions, or they've gone through traumas, or they've made other choices in their life where they are lingering around. Some of them simply don't know how to move on.

So they hang out at places or with people where they think they can benefit. Sometimes they hang around coffee shops, if they have a coffee addiction. They might hang around porn shops if they had a sex addiction. They might hang around someone who has certain behaviors that they're attracted to.

Every bit of energy on this Earth, even the emotions that we have, operate at a certain vibration. Those energies attract other energies. I see some of this going on when I walk through an airport. I can see and feel those disembodied and unclean spirits on a mass scale in the airports when you have so many people in small space.

They will gravitate towards certain individuals. Sometimes those unclean disembodied spirits will gravitate toward a person of the light, because they're actually trying to find the light but they don't know how to get there. They don't know how to actually go to the True Source, the Savior Jesus Christ.

They might hang around someone like that so they can feed off of their light energy. They are a bit like vampires actually. I don't mean that in the literal sense, but symbolically speaking, they suck the energy out of people. That's where those spirit attachments come in.

Eric: That's interesting. I guess the question is how do we know if we have them around us? I know a girl right now, a sweet girl. She has suicidal thoughts at times. She has dark thoughts and often goes into periods of depression. I've come to believe that those things come from the devil. They come from the adversary.

We shouldn't say "the devil made me do it" but I do believe that the devil, or those who work with him, are around us, giving us thoughts like, "You have no value, you should end your life, you don't have friends, you're worthless."

Julie: Absolutely they do. They will speak into your thoughts, and they will put dark thought energy in there. It's just a different form of matter. Thoughts, words, and actions are all different degrees of matter that impacts us.

When I was on the other side of the veil, we weren't talking with our mouths. It was very telepathic. Even with the animals, the grass and the trees, it was a telepathic communication. It was as if we could read each other's minds.

So absolutely they put thought energy in there. Sometimes you might hear it as an actual voice, but most of the time it is a thought impression that is put into the mind. They also use different types of energy weapons that can affect the mind, body, and spirit. I have experienced this in every level. I have had suicidal thoughts.

When I woke up, I was *so* sick and depressed because I missed the other side of the veil so much. I've come to understand that I had so many demons and disembodied spirits that were working on me trying to depress me at that time. I knew it wasn't my own thoughts, but I felt powerless to combat them. I felt absolutely outnumbered. I felt like I didn't have the tools or the weapons in *my* arsenal to be able to fight against the darkest demons that were there to destroy me.

I am here to spread Light and tell people that you absolutely do! You do have that power. We have weapons of Light that are just as good, and even better, than the weapons of darkness. We have flaming white swords, for instance, that can cut through some of the worst mucky muck that is out there. It is amazing to me to see, as we shield ourselves and put on our Armor of God, how much that alone can protect us from these adversarial influences.

Eric: Interesting. You're making a scriptural phrase come to mind related to spiritual warfare and weaponry: "the fiery darts of the adversary."

Julie: Right. Those are real.

Eric: So that's a scriptural, doctrinal concept. I like that.

Julie: In Ephesians in the Bible, they talk about putting on the Armor of God. Putting on the whole armor. Right now as I say, "Putting on the Armor of God," I guarantee you the majority of the people listening will automatically have an image of some form of armor that is on them. They will have their favorite armor.

It is my understanding that the armor they had, even premortally, they designed themselves. It is absolutely real, it is not imagined, and it is absolutely critical that you put on the Armor of God.

Imagine every day that you put it on, and you pray for that armor. You cover your head, you cover your hands, your fingers, your toes, and your whole body. Then you ask and invoke the power of God through the Authority of Jesus Christ and ask for that armor to be put on. You will find that it will not completely protect you all of the time, but you will find an increase in power and protection against those who would seek to hurt you.

Eric: What about those who feel that only men who hold certain religious, spiritual, or priesthood powers have the ability to command dark spirits. What do you think?

Julie: Well, that's one of the biggest lies. Satan would love it if only a handful of men on this planet could take care of the demons, because he knows there's no way they can. But the minute a man or a woman or a child realizes his divine origin, his divine potential, and his divine power to know that he can cast them out and can invite the unclean spirits to go to the Light, the more power they have.

Knowledge is power. Make sure we get knowledge from the right source, but it is absolutely the first point of defense in being able to combat the enemy.

Eric: What do I tell this friend of mine who has suicidal thoughts? I want to say to her, "Every time you have a dark thought, or you feel like your life has no value, you can be assured, every time, that there is a devil near you, or within you, giving you those messages."

Julie: That is true. It's either a devil or an unclean spirit, and often it's both. The devils will utilize the unclean spirits. They will actually put them under contract. They will coerce them, they will convince them that they are worthless, that they themselves are in bondage because of actions they participated in, or because of their own unworthiness or inability to discern truth from error. They are to this day and at this moment utilizing and recruiting unclean spirits to be able to try to fight the Light.

I'm here to tell you that I have never seen or heard of anyone who has experienced suicidal thoughts or any dark feelings of depression or despair without there being actual demons and unclean spirits who are involved in that.

I say that because I struggle with depression. I've struggled with anxiety and despair energy, and I'm no better than anyone else. I have struggled with it because that is part of the test of mortality for me.

I understand that the dark spirits have their assignments. On the other side of the veil in the Heavens, things are patterned. God's pattern is we have the Godhead of God the Father, the Son Jesus Christ, and the Holy Spirit. Then there are Councils. There is a Council of Twelve that extends out to other quorums and councils.

That same pattern is used here on Earth, and that same pattern is mimicked by Satan and the dark side. They did it premortally, and they do it on the Earth. They have people who have made dark oaths and are Satanic worshipers here on the Earth. They have been enlisted in Satan's cause, and he uses that same pattern in the Spirit Realm.

They are powerful, but they are not more powerful than God. God is light years ahead. Light energy accelerates, dark energy decelerates. The two cannot coincide. Dark energy does not create, it manipulates. Light energy is where Creation comes from.

So everything on the dark side is mimicking the Light. It's counterfeit, it's not lasting, and it only ends in destruction. Ultimately, Satan himself will be destroyed in the Final Battle.

Who am I to say that, right? I'm just Julie Rowe. What authority does Julie Rowe have? I'll tell you the authority I have. I am an endowed Daughter of God who speaks in behalf of Christ because I love Him, and I committed to be a member of His Church.

I know without a doubt that He has given me power to combat this enemy and therefore I have an accountability to Him and to my brothers and sisters to witness and testify. As part of our mortal ministries, we agreed premortally to go through these tests and to be subjected to the adversary as we need to. But that does not mean that we just lay down and let him kick us.

It means we get up and do everything the Lord has given us to be able to combat this. The biggest weapon the Lord has given us that we can use against Satan is love. Truth and love. That is the biggest weapon. He hates it. You wanna talk about the gnashing of teeth? That'll make him thrash. He absolutely cannot stand it when I testify of love.

We can combat all day long with weapons of negative energy against negative energy, but we will get nowhere with that. Where we get progress is when we send people to the Light.

We express our love, then we stand firm in that belief and we say: "Listen, I don't have to take this!" We send love, even as they persecute us. They despise it. It takes their power away.

Eric: What would you tell the millions of people in the world who are depressed, having feelings of lack of self-worth and want to end their lives? Their lives are hard, and they don't have friends. What would you say to help them pull out of this?

Julie: Well, one of the basics is to pray to God the Father in the name of Jesus Christ with all of your might, mind, and strength for deliverance. Anyone can do this, whether they're of Christian faith or otherwise. This is basic. You will find deliverance immediately if in the name of Jesus Christ you expose and reveal them, and you rebuke them.

But rebuking them comes at a different cost, versus if you invite unclean spirits to the Light. I love missionary work. I see missionary work happening on the other side of the veil, and the gathering is going on there. So if we could have more of our brothers and sisters join the forces of Light, why wouldn't we do that?

If we are new at this and just starting out, we don't need to try to discern right away which energy is which. It's gonna be confusing for people to try to tell is this an unclean disembodied spirit, or is this a devil?

I think it's much more productive to just invite them to the Light. If you're still being bombarded or mobbed, though, you identify that as a purposeful attack. Know from the beginning that they have people assigned as depression demons, suicidal demons, murder demons, divorce demons, despair demons, and everything you can think of.

They have their assignments and their whole goal is to make you suffer. If someone on the dark side is assigned to make someone depressed, that is their assignment.

They hound you, and they hound you. So if you recognize that there is a real enemy, even though you can't see them, that is your first line of defense.

It is then time to strategize. A good strategy is to first put on that Armor, second pray to the Lord and ask for Christ to deliver you, and third, if they're not leaving you alone, you tell them to get away from you.

Eric: There's a lot of power in our speech and the things we say. I believe that just simply uttering statements of happiness, joy, love, peace, or even using Jesus Christ's name out loud has power against them. Do you agree?

Julie: Absolutely it does. Also, when you tell them to get away, you don't just leave that energy open. You then invite Light to surround you, and you ask for additional Ministering Angels.

I appreciate that you said that, Eric, because there's loose ends that have to be tied up when you're clearing out dark energy. You don't wanna leave a void. Ask for additional Ministering Angels to come in.

If you ask, you'll have your Guardian Angels, your righteous ancestors, and others come in and fill that void with Light energy and protection. When you do that, there are billions of spirits on the other side of the veil that are waiting to help us.

Due to agency and due to the way that the Lord organizes His Kingdom, He'll send people who are assigned to us, but if we want additional help and we really want to invoke the power of the Priesthood for protection, we need to ask for that. We need to spread Love and Light, and we need to ask for Love and Light to come into our lives.

Eric: That's great. Thanks for that, Julie. You just mentioned ancestors and those on the other side who are *for* us. Now that's a different topic and I'm wondering if you'd like to do an episode on the Heavenly Help and those on the other side who are in it for our best interest?

Julie: I would love that. I'd like to end on a positive note anyway, so that we're not leaving that yucky energy out there. I think that would be great, Eric, to do an entire podcast just on

Ministering and Guardian Angels, and how wonderful they are, and how we can ask for that help.

The Lord hasn't left us alone in a desert to starve and die. He has actually been sending us Messengers. They intervene in our lives more than we know. If we had any idea how much they are going to combat for us, I think it would be astounding. If our eyes could be unveiled, we could actually see what's going on in these different dimensions.

I have had glimpses of that in mortality, and it does make you crazy. You don't wanna see that all the time. The veil is a blessing. But when it comes to that Light energy and those Ministering Angels, they are so beautiful and they're so amazing. Why would we not wanna call upon them for help? Unless it's just our own pride.

Anyway. It's amazing. I love it. I think we should do a podcast on that. That's a great idea, Eric.

Eric: Sounds good. Well, we have the Scriptures and a lot of resources for learning about these things, but I just want to thank you again for sharing your visionary gifts. The insights you've had regarding the other side of the veil are a blessing to me and to many others.

Julie: Eric, thank you. I express gratitude to everyone who's listening and can spread Light wherever you go, knowing that there is real power in Faith in Christ and real power in knowing we can combat the enemy and we can do all things through Christ. I have a witness and a testimony of this.

I know with a hundred percent surety. I know that God is over all. He has a Plan, and we are not alone. I wish you the best for your day today.

I hope that as you put on your Armor of God and look around you, and you see with open eyes more so than you did a few minutes ago, you'll realize that we are physical temporal beings living in a spiritual world and not the other way around. We are spiritual beings, living in a temporal world. We've gotta switch that energy and make sure that people know that we were created spiritually before we ever had a body.

Don't let Satan fool you one bit. He is absolutely jealous that he doesn't have a body. He's doing everything he can to try to keep you from realizing your Divine Potential, because he doesn't want you to have what he will never have, which is to live at home in a glorious mansion in Heaven. And this I say in Christ's name, Amen.

PODCAST 5

❧

GETTING TO KNOW JULIE ROWE

Julie: Hi folks! Welcome to the Julie Rowe show. I've got Eric Smith on the line and I'm in for a surprise today. Let's find out what he has in store for us. Hi Eric!

Eric: Hey Julie. I hope you're ready to be grilled just a little bit because I have some questions for you.

Julie: Should I be nervous?

Eric: Yes, you probably should be a little bit, to be honest!

Julie: (laughing) All right!

Eric: I was sitting here, just minutes ago. We had another topic planned and I decided to shake things up. I know that some of your listeners have interests other than future things and prophecy. I know that you have a number of listeners who care deeply for you and would like to get to know you a little better. So I thought of a few questions. I'm kind of planning on inspiration as it comes to give you enough questions about yourself to create an entire podcast out of this. Does that sound okay?

Julie: Sure. I've said that I would be willing to answer questions of any guest as best I can, and you have picked a topic that I know quite a bit about!

I can't wiggle my way out of it, because I agreed to this and I said in the very first podcast that these would be live recordings and any questions that the guest asks, I will succumb to. That's part of the fun of doing these. So go for it, Eric.

Eric: Great! I'm glad you see it my way.

Julie: If it's too personal I'm going to tell you, "That's none of your business!"

Eric: That's okay, but no guarantees! I'm gonna ask anything that comes to my mind.

Julie: Well, this is good. It'll mix up the energy a little bit too because some of these podcasts we've been doing are so intense, right?

Eric: It's time for a change!

Julie: (laughing) Wake up! Wake up people! Well, we talked about how it would be fun to do a comical podcast or two so people can see my weird sense of humor. I don't want them to think I'm just always intense or that I'm always in Spirit Mode. They can understand that I have a really strange sense of humor and I like to joke around a lot.

It's like my sense of humor is a coping strategy, so maybe this could be the comical one. We could laugh at me and how I cope with things in my life. I'm game.

Eric: Well, let's start with some basics here and get them out of the way. Tell us your favorite color.

Julie: Oh, you would start with that. I don't have a favorite color because I like all the colors of the rainbow and I can never decide. So it depends on my mood that day, and what I wanna wear. If I had to narrow it down to just one color it would probably be navy blue, or just blue in general. I love greens. I like all the bright colors.

I tend to go for more of the winter colors, the more bold colors when I'm wearing things, because I have dark hair. So, I don't know if that answers it well enough. But I have never been able to decide, ever since I was a little girl, what my favorite color was.

Eric: Okay, fair enough. Let's move on. Let's try another basic here. What is your favorite kind of food? Like, if you're gonna go eat out.

Julie: People are gonna notice a theme here, Eric. (laughs) I can't decide! It depends on what my mood is and what I wanna eat. I will say that Jeff and I, when we go out to dinner, we like to go to restaurants where we can't make that kind of food on our own. So we tend to go to restaurants like that. I love Thai food, I love Indian food. Those are probably my top two favorites - Thai food and Indian food. I never seem to get enough Pad Thai, I just gotta say that.

Eric: (laughing)

Julie: We like our regular burger joints and stuff like that, but I don't tend to usually go out for a burger. I like Italian restaurants, but Jeff prefers to not go there because he feels we can easily make Italian food at our house. I love Chinese food, too, even though I know that it's not always the best for you, in the American method of making it.

I love to eat out, as is evidenced by the fact that I have gained about fifty pounds in the three years of going public with my story. I've been on the road so much, and I've been eating out a lot. Then, just as a stress relief, I've gone out to dinner with my husband on dates and stuff. It's showing in my physique, but it's been worth it!

Eric: Well, it happens to the best of us! Let's keep it on the food theme for a minute . . .

Julie: I'm also over forty. I'm forty-four now. My birthday was in January and so that probably has something to do with my metabolism slowing down. Anyway, the food thing . . .

Eric: (laughs) Excuses, excuses.

Julie: Hey, I work out every day! Monday through Friday! Almost. There are a few days I don't. That makes me wanna sing that song "I Work Out." Anyway, go ahead. (laughing)

Eric: All right, let's keep it on food for a minute. That's an area that I'm really comfortable in. When you're at home, what is a meal that you like to prepare for the family?

Julie: Well, I'm glad you said that I "like" to prepare because I don't usually like to prepare meals. That's the role my husband likes to do. I like to keep it easy.

My kids would tell you that we eat spaghetti way too much. I love spaghetti. I have a really good spaghetti sauce that I make. I like angel hair pasta. So that's probably my number one "go to" meal because you can make it quickly, it tastes good, it goes with a good caesar salad, a couple of breadsticks with some corn on the side. You know, get all that pasta and starch, and the carbs. (laughing)

I make some good enchiladas. My husband, on the other hand, just in the last month came up with a recipe for his own beef and broccoli, and it is tasty. He also is really good at making an Asian chicken. So if we wanna go with the really good cooking, that's Jeff.

Eric: Would your kids agree?

Julie: Yes, they would. They tell me I'm a good cook, but they tell Jeff he's a great cook. (laughing)

Eric: Well, since you've introduced your husband to us, what can you tell us about him?

Julie: I think he's totally hot. (laughing) I'm madly in love with him. He's gonna be so embarrassed if he hears this, but I'm shouting it out to the world!

We got married in April of 1996, and what can I tell about him? He's tall, dark, and handsome, and he is absolutely been one of my greatest strengths. He's stood by my side. He's witty, he's strong, he's hard working. He is diligent and is obedient to the Lord's commandments.

I could do an entire podcast on Jeff Rowe. Maybe that's what we should do. Nobody knows who my husband is. They're always like, "Who's the mysterious man by that woman?" We could do an entire podcast on just Jeff Rowe.

Eric: I'm sure he'd love that.

Julie: The man behind the scenes (singing).

Eric: Okay, keeping with family life, what can you say about your children?

Julie: My children. Ethan, Spencer, and Aubrianna. Ethan just graduated from high school a couple of weeks ago, and he's getting ready to put his mission papers in for the Church of Jesus Christ of Latter-day Saints. He's eighteen.

Spencer is gonna be a junior in high school. He's sixteen.

Aubrianna is thirteen. She just finished seventh grade, she'll be in eighth grade this fall. I have awesome kids. They turned out beautiful, but better yet, they are Christlike, loving, and good children. They love me a lot, and they are really good to me, most of the time. Although they do typical teenage things, like, telling me I'm embarrassing. To which I say: "Isn't that my job?! I'm your mom!"

Eric: I'd like to push a little farther on that last comment and ask you to give an example of a time you've embarrassed Aubri.

Julie: Well, when her friends come over I talk in different accents and voices. Her friends think it's really funny and cool, but she wants to hide. I'm not very good at accents, but I'm trying to practice. I do have one I could do for people.

Eric: I think you should go ahead and do that.

Julie: People are gonna be totally embarrassed for me, because I'm no good at it. Just realize that I'm a beginner when it comes to these accents. In no way am I pretending to be someone I'm not, and in no way would I ever wanna offend anybody in the South. But I'm (speaking with an accent) practicin' my gator huntin' voice, cause I love gators and I'm gunna…

No, I can't do it for real! When I actually have a real audience, I can't do it! It's too embarrassing!

(speaking in an accent) "Whaddya say, you en me, we go out an get us some gators?"

This is why Aubri gets embarrassed, because I will say: (speaking in an accent) "Hey honey lamb! I'm so good yer over here! Why don't you bring yer friends in the kitchen fer some ice cream?"

As I said, her friends think I'm hilariously funny, and Aubri just wants to hide because she's like: "Oh my gosh, my mom's a dork."

I will be the first to tell you that I am! Yes, I am a big nerd.

Eric: Well, after that accent, I'd just like to give my sympathies to Aubri.

Julie: You haven't seen anything yet. You should get my British accent or some of my other accents that I come up with. Again, I'm totally awful at them, but I do it because it de-stresses me. Plus, I've found with my kids sometimes when they're frustrating me, I'll use humor so that I don't get mad.

I still get mad, but so that I don't totally lose it, sometimes I go into my weird accent mode so that I can tell them things like: (speaking in her gator huntin' voice again) "Boy! I told you a hundred times to put that video game away and get your chores done!"

I find that, every now and then, they actually listen better if I don't use my real voice.

Eric: Well, there's a little tip for all of your listeners!

Julie: Then again, if they're gonna tune you out, they tune you out. There's nothing you can do a lot of the time. Anyway, I try.

Eric: Okay, tell me what an average weekend is like, or a typical day in the life of the Rowe family.

Julie: My husband and my kids would say that I'm on the phone all the time. I agree. I would say since starting this mission, especially starting GTRF, The Greater Tomorrow Relief Fund, which I founded in 2015, I am on the phone like ninety percent of the time.

I'm on the phone a lot. That gets on my family's nerves. I constantly tell them: "It's my job! This is what I do."

I would love to talk in person to everyone, but I live in the country, in a house by myself when the kids go to school, and I get to talk on the phone and do work when I'm not traveling. The way that I do the relief effort work is by connecting people on the phone. So yes, I'm on the phone a lot.

I have started doing energy sessions again. That's been fun. It has been really great to be able to help people with some of the things that they're dealing with.

Then, I travel. I've been traveling about a week a month during the last couple of years to spread the message and to work on GTRF, the relief effort. So they're getting pretty tired of me traveling, but they're a good support to me.

As far as the kids go, my oldest has been playing basketball and football, my second son wrestles and plays football, and my daughter sings in the chorale. She's got a great singing voice. All of the kids have taken piano, although none of them are taking lessons right now.

So I'm busy with the typical mom stuff that you have when you've got teenagers. They go to Church youth activities on Wednesday night, and we go to Church on Sunday for three hours. Then every once in awhile I get a nap.

I don't usually take naps, but if I get tired enough and slow down, I'll take a nap every now and then. My husband takes a Sunday nap almost every Sunday, but that depends on his calling and whether or not he's able to do that. Let's see, the rest of the week we eat breakfast, lunch, and dinner.

Eric: (laughs)

Julie: I don't know. We have extended family. My husband's family is in the Kansas City area, most of them, his siblings. We get together with his family about once a month on average, sometimes twice a month depending on how many birthdays there are, or for the holidays and stuff like that.

Eric: What do you and Jeff and the kids like to do together?

Julie: We like to go out to eat, and we have moved out to the country. We live about fifteen minutes from the small town here, and so there's not a lot to do. We have some decent sized restaurants in town, and a Walmart, and a few clothing stores and shoe stores, but other than that, we go up to the Kansas City area.

I'm not a huge shopper. I really don't like to shop. I'm one of those people that if I need something I go get it, much to my daughter's dismay. She loves to shop and wishes I was the kind of mom that would take her shopping.

The one thing I do for myself is to get my nails done. So every now and then I get a pedicure. I get my nails done every two to three weeks. That's my one place that I spoil myself.

As a family we like to go to all the kids events and games together. We like to camp, although we haven't done that this year, just due to our busy schedules. We like to take a family vacation in the summer. I took the kids to Destin, Florida for spring break with a friend, and that was fun. We're gonna have a family reunion with my husband's family, so we're looking forward to that.

We like to play board games and we like to play card games. My husband loves the game Skip Bo. So we play Skip Bo, Apples to Apples, you know, the typical things that most families do. We're not really that unusual.

Eric: Okay, let's change gears here. Let's go back to the young Julie and tell your listeners what you were like as a girl. Were you a rabble rouser? Were you a goody goody? What kind of person was the young Julie Rowe?

Julie: I'm really glad you qualified it to young, like an adolescent teenager, because I was gonna give you a bad time for calling me old at the age of forty-four.

Eric: (laughing)

Julie: What, are you trying to say I'm old?! I'm forty-four with a body that's so beat up I'm like I'm in my seventies. Well, you wanna break it down to like the adolescent years? It changed for me as I went through some of the stages, so. . .

Eric: Let's start with grade school, up to high school age.

Julie: Okay. In grade school I was really shy. From kindergarten through second and third grade, I was really timid. I was easily influenced by adults and I absolutely never wanted to disappoint any of them. I was a people pleaser.

I had a hard time speaking up for myself when I was uncomfortable or didn't agree with what somebody was doing. By about fourth to sixth grade I started getting involved in student government at school, and I started finding a little bit of a niche for myself in leadership roles.

I was elected in fourth grade as a class representative, fifth grade as Vice President, and sixth grade as President of my elementary. My siblings tease me to this day that my glory days were in sixth grade when I could run the school.

Eric: (laughing)

Julie: It's actually been years since we talked about it. Probably about ten or twelve years ago we had a family reunion I was in charge of, and we had a good laugh about that.

So I had natural leadership abilities. I found early on when we lived in Hawaii that I had a really big problem when people were being abused, mistreated, or bullied in any way. So I would take a stand against bullies, and therefore get bullied sometimes.

Again, I consider myself a recovering people pleaser. I'm still working on not being a people pleaser. In the sense that I have had to learn how to say no to people. There's a lot of reasons for that, but learning how to say no, and going public with my story has forced me to do that, because I've had so many people wanting attention or wanting to ask me things of a personal nature.

It has forced me to learn how to discern what I can and can't say, or who to say it to, or who to trust or not trust. I'm learning it's okay to not be able to please everyone.

So I would say that was one of my biggest personality qualities was always wanting to please people, not wanting to let people down. But mostly, I just have a really big heart and I don't ever want anyone to hurt. If there's anything I can do to take that hurt or pain away, that's a big motivator for me.

Eric: Interesting. Please tell us what your grades were like.

Julie: Mostly A's and a couple B's. I got a C in high school, in algebra II, for one semester.

Eric: What were your favorite subjects?

Julie: I loved biology, I loved earth science, I loved English. I liked math until I got into algebra II and then I had a teacher I didn't care for, and the same with trigonometry. Those two teachers were really not pleasant. I was bored out of my mind in those classes because of the way that it was taught, but I liked math really well up until my sophomore and junior years in high school.

I liked chemistry, but I didn't really care for my chemistry teacher. Nothing against her, but her teaching style was boring to me. But I liked the sciences a lot. I would say the sciences were my favorite, because I loved geography. I absolutely loved geography and I liked studying rock formations and things like that.

Eric: Cool.

Julie: I always loved the arts. I didn't take any art classes in high school or college because of feeling like I had to take more serious classes for my resume. So I took computer classes and web design, and things like that, because I was attracted to the business classes. I was in Business Honor Society in high school.

Eric: When you went to college tell us about your major there. Or maybe a little about your social life, or anything that stands out from your college years.

Julie: Well, this is gonna be very telling for people. They'll recognize a theme in my behavior. I like so many things that I often have a hard time deciding what I like the best, and that was exactly what happened to me when I was at BYU.

Every semester I tried to figure out what my major was gonna be, but I wanted to take so many different classes. I didn't wanna have to narrow it down to one field of study, and a lot of the majors that I wanted to participate in required internships or travel abroad that required more money, or unpaid training.

I left home at eighteen. I came home for one month after my freshman year, and then I never lived at home after that. So I was supporting myself. It was really hard, because I was forced to choose a major that I could do quickly and that didn't require an internship or something like that.

So I was limited in what I could do just because of a financial obligation. I was really drawn to Recreation Management. I thought that would be a super cool major. I thought Communications would be a fun major. I thought that Accounting would be cool until I saw that I had to take calculus, and I didn't wanna take calculus. (laughs)

I got a high enough score on my ACT at BYU that they waived my college algebra. I either had to take four years of a foreign language, or take calculus or statistics. I ended up taking statistics and that's what passed my math off.

To this day I've never taken calculus and I'm glad! But I find it interesting that in dreams and night visions I have been shown calculus. So I've never taken a class on Earth in calculus, but in night visions I have been taught calculus. Same thing with physics. I never took a physics class but I've been shown physics. So I actually have a knowledge about physics and calculus, but it's not because I learned it in an Earthly institution.

Eric: Hmm. Now I wanna just slightly change topics and just ask you about your spirituality in all of those years. From a young girl up to your college years. What was your religious life like?

Julie: Well, I was raised in the Church of Jesus Christ of Latter-day Saints, which is the LDS faith. My dad was an LDS Chaplain in the military, meaning he was basically a representative of the LDS Church.

So from the time I was a little girl, he had what we called, "Dad's Work Church" and that was where, as a Chaplain, he performed nondenominational services. From my earliest recollection of four and five years old, we would go to the Post Chapel where they did Protestant or nondenominational services that he would lead.

Sometimes other Chaplains would lead or they'd do them together, and I would sit in those meetings for about an hour. So we'd be there for about an hour and a half, if you count the punch and cookies, right? We always had red punch.

Eric: (laughing)

Julie: I remember my parents being worried that I was gonna spill red punch on my Church dress, or that my brothers would spill it on their dress shirts. They would always tell us we could only have two cookies (laughs). We had so many kids that they didn't want to be embarrassed if we hoarded all the cookies every Sunday.

Eric: How many kids were there?

Julie: Well, we ended up with ten kids. I'm the second of ten. My parents had a kid just about every two years. The oldest is eighteen years and a day apart from my youngest sister. Some were sixteen months apart, some were twenty-eight months apart, but all within about a two-year time frame. So that's a lot of kids.

I take my hat off to my parents, because it's one thing to take your kids to church once a week for an hour and a half, but we would also attend meetings at our LDS church, which was three hours long. We would go to Sacrament Meeting, when the whole congregation met together. Then I would go to what they call Primary for the children, which was forty minutes. Then after a break we'd have Sunday School which was another forty minutes, or Singing Time. So I got three hours of the LDS faith every Sunday, and then about an hour and a half at the other church.

By the time we got ready for Church, went to Church, went to our congregation and the other one, it was about six to seven hours of church-related activities on Sunday during those years.

Eric: So you had exposure to other faiths?

Julie: Yes I did. Because of that, there were a lot of faiths that would come and go in that chapel, before or after. The Catholic congregations would come in before or after the Presbyterians and Episcopalians. Then also on occasion I went with friends when I was in junior high, but mostly in high school. In high school I went to several different congregations.

I always went to the LDS faith, though. That was where my understanding, my belief and my testimony was, as far as understanding some of the gospel principles that I had been raised with.

I went at least once to Presbyterian, Episcopalian, Baptist, and Southern Baptist meetings. I've been in a Jewish Synagogue, although I've never actually attended Synagogue. I've just been where they actually practice it. I learned a great deal about the main Christian faiths in my personal studies.

Starting when I was about thirteen, I read the Book of Mormon for the first time. At that point in time I started branching out in my belief system to try to understand other faiths and other denominations.

I had a lot of friends that were not LDS. In seventh grade I was the only Mormon in my school of two thousand, and in eighth grade I had a small group of LDS friends, and then in high school. So I was used to being the odd one out and being different. There was a part of me that kind of liked that, because it strengthened my testimony and my resolve for my own faith. Plus, I learned very early on that a lot of people don't like Mormons. (laughs)

It helped motivate me to ask, "Why don't they like me, just because I'm Mormon?" It forced me to ask tough questions at a young age. By the time I was thirteen I read the Book of Mormon because of things going on in my personal life, as well as being at a point where I had heard the story about Joseph Smith.

I heard that he was fourteen when he saw God the Father and the Savior in the grove of trees in New York. And I had a very strong testimony from a young age about Christ and the things that I'd been taught.

I was baptized in the LDS faith when I was eight years old, and I had a very strong witness when I was baptized that I was being obedient to God. When I had my interview with my Bishop, the Spirit was so strong, my heart was so tender at the age of eight, that I cried in that interview. I was so happy that I got to be baptized, and I knew that I was doing a good thing.

So my progression in the Gospel and my understanding of doctrine and principles came line upon line, and it was also assisted from those on the other side of the veil that would come and strengthen me. It also came with a lot of opposition early on.

Eric: What was it like to be in a military family? You did a lot of traveling, I assume.

Julie: We did. There were good things and bad things about it. It was really hard to give up my toys and other belongings when we would move, to try to make weight limits. We had a large family and they only give you so much weight that you're allowed to have when you move that they'll pay for.

It's based on rank, not on how many kids you have in your family. So if you have six kids, they make you meet weight limit and anything you go over on your weight limit, you have to pay for, and it's expensive. So my parents were always getting rid of things. We were always cleaning house.

When I was younger that was really hard, but that was just one thing that affected me emotionally as a kid. The benefit of that was that I learned not to be attached to things, but instead to be attached to my family and to be attached to the relationships that really matter, rather than being attached to a house or a school or a community, or my toys.

I also learned that it's really important to do spring cleaning. My mom would go through things every three to four months and clean out, and I do the same thing. Every three to four months, sometimes six months at the most, I go through my house and I just get rid of things that we don't need that are cluttering things up. Because of that, I keep a clean house. I don't like clutter. (laughing)

Eric: Yeah. In all the places you lived growing up, and being part of a military family, what were some of the more memorable locations or places you lived?

Julie: I liked each place for different reasons. I lived the longest in Texas, but I was super young there. Then Washington, Hawaii, and Germany. Those were my three favorite places.

Each one was unique. Washington state is totally different than Hawaii, and Hawaii is totally different than Germany. But I was able to build memories in those places and establish myself with friends.

Then in between that, we have Texas, California, New Jersey, New York, and then during my junior and senior year of high school, and after the summer of my freshman year at BYU, my family lived in northern Virginia.

My dad worked at the Pentagon. That was not my favorite place because of all the politicians and military people that are out there. I felt high stress and a lot of the corruption and dark energy when I was there, with some of the gifts I have. That is also where some of the breakdown of my family happened, prior to my parents' divorce.

So I had a lot more painful experiences when I lived in northern

Virginia. That is where I started having more intense dreams and visions about the big earthquake that's coming to Utah.

Eric: That leads me into the next question that I wanted to ask. A lot of your listeners know that you've had a Near Death Experience, but a lot of them may not know that you've had more than one, and they started at a young age. Can you say anything about leaving your body?

Julie: I would have dreams and visions from early on. I don't remember being on this planet without having dreams and visions, or without having visitations from the other side. I would either smell visitors or sense them or feel them.

Every once in awhile I would see them with my eyes. I would more often see them with my spirit eyes. I would feel someone near me, and then I would get a visual of them in my mind. The Spirit would then make known to me who was visiting. I've had that gift for as long as I can remember, and it just kind of grew exponentially as my capabilities and my understanding developed.

It just accelerated after I had my 2004 NDE. The veil became more thin, I guess, but the first out-of-body experience I had was when I was seven. I had surgery for my tonsils and adenoids to be removed.

Then I had one in fifth grade. I had foot surgery, and I had an out of body experience during that surgery as well. We talk about that in the biography so I'm not gonna go into detail on that. I don't think we talked about others in the book, did we? Other than the ones after 2004?

Eric: Not as a young person. I think the next one we mentioned was 2004.

Julie: Yeah. In 2004, I had two and a half days on the other side of the veil. I was very sick. We talk about that in my book *A Greater Tomorrow*, and the second book *The Time is Now*. I also wrote

From Tragedy to Destiny, which is written to a non-denominational audience and is a compilation of the first two books, with some more clarification and other details that are not in the first two books.

I talk about my Near Death Experience in *A Greater Tomorrow*, and that was when I was thirty one years old. I'd been married about eight years and my youngest daughter was eight and a half months old. So I'm coming up on the thirteen year anniversary.

Sometimes I refer to it as a reunion, because I got to see family members on the other side of the veil. I had that one in September, another one in October, then a smaller one in November of that same year.

In July 2005 I had an out of body experience, and then after going public with my story in 2014, I have had at least four where I was on death's door. I had such severe adversarial attacks from going public with my story that there would be times I was in bed for anywhere from five to seven days, just trying to recover from all the negative energy that was coming at me.

I had another major one after the Ogden Energy Conference in 2015. Then I had one just this last October of 2016.

Eric: What I've learned in talking to you about these experiences is they all vary in their length, in their depth, and in the understanding that came to you. I was really interested in your last one in 2016, where you received some doctrinally profound insights. Is there anything else that you wanna say about your NDE's, overall?

Julie: I will say that they are difficult to go through. They're life-changing, and they're painful, coming in and out of the body like that. I wouldn't wish it on my worst enemy, because they're that difficult, but I know that they've been a blessing to me. The learning and understanding I've gained has come at a cost, though, due to the physical, mental, and emotional pain that comes with it.

When we're given knowledge, we have a choice to act on that

knowledge or not. The more of these experiences I have had, the more clarity and understanding I've been given, the more I'm accountable to God. Which is why I speak so boldly today.

Eric: One of those costs you pay is a cost that comes to you and your family. How has having these experiences the last several years of your life affected your family and your ability to live a normal life?

Julie: It's been difficult. Right now my kids are supportive, but they're sick of hearing about it. They're regular kids. They wanna have a regular life. They wanna be able to just have a normal mom, and I'm far from normal, whatever normal is. I can't hide who I am, and I don't wanna hide who I am. I wanna be who I am.

I wanna speak openly as I can with as many people who'll listen, but there are a lot of personal things I keep to myself. I don't share everything, not even close. I only share a small portion of what I feel the Spirit can allow me to do.

I have purposely kept my kids out of the limelight. I have purposely not put pictures of them on the internet, knowing that all these years later we would be at this point.

I've purposely not brought them to functions or speaking events, and the same goes with my husband. He is my protector and my provider, but I am extremely private and extremely protective of him and of his privacy. He has been magnificent in his support of me, although it's been difficult on our marriage ever since I woke up in 2004.

My health issues have caused anguish for him and for my loved ones. It's been difficult, and it has weighed very heavily on his heart and on that of my children. You can only imagine as a husband, or as children, to watch your wife or your mother be as sick as I have been again and again, and not have it affect you on an emotional and mental level.

Eric: Okay, I wanna lighten things with one or two more

questions. What is your favorite candybar? I can't believe we missed this! (laughing)

Julie: Baby Ruth! Baby Ruth. (laughing) Although I love Snickers and Twix too. I love Whoppers. But if I had to pick one, if there was only one candy bar to choose on the planet, it would be Baby Ruth. If anybody that wants to mail me some Baby Ruths that *aren't* poisoned, have at it!

Eric: (laughing) That's great!

Julie: My mailing address is P.O. Box 895, Ottawa, Kansas, 66067. I say that because that is my mailing address and I'm not afraid to give it out now, whereas I used to be. I figure if somebody wants to send me something that is not nice, that's what the Post Office is for. (laughing)

They can filter through it before they put it in my box! Also, if you wanna make donations to GTRF, you can either go online or send it directly there, if you'd rather send to that. You can put it to GTRF, or if you wanna write me a letter, I'm good with that. I need as much encouragement as possible and I'm tired of just getting bills in the mail, quite frankly.

Eric: So there you go, listeners. Please write Julie a letter of encouragement. I think it would be really nice.

Julie: Plus, if you send snail mail, I don't have to print them out from my computer. I can save them for my scrapbooks, because that's the only thing I care about. Right now, I could walk away from everything I own, except for my pictures and my letters. I will keep your letters if you send them, I promise.

Eric: Julie, this has been fun. Thank you for opening up and sharing a little more of your personal side. I just think you're a wonderful person and a lot of fun, and very normal. I'm grateful for your friendship. Thanks for sharing your life with us.

Julie: Thank you, Eric. It's very nice of you to take the time to help with these podcasts. We appreciate all of your work. That's all, folks! Have a great day.

PODCAST 6

WHAT I SEE IN THE WESTERN UNITED STATES

Julie: We'd like to welcome you to the Julie Rowe Show today. I have my friend Eric helping us and also my friend Joel who's gonna be guiding some of the questions we have today. Today's topic is: "What I see in the United States." We're gonna focus on a few of the regions in the United States and see where we go.

Joel, welcome. How are you today?

Joel: Great, Julie. Thanks for having me.

Julie: Thank you for being here. Eric, we'd like to welcome you as well. Thanks again for your help on everything.

I'm pretty excited about this podcast because there are so many things that I see around the world, and particularly in the United States. I've had thousands of emails come in, and several hundred emails specifically asked questions about what I see around the world and in the United States in particular.

The questions range from where the foreign troops will come in, the type of warfare we're gonna be involved in, the natural disasters, plagues, and other things. They also ask about the topic of The Gathering and the mission of The Greater Tomorrow Relief Fund. So today's broadcast is gonna be focusing on questions that

Joel has relating to what I see in the United States.

Like the other podcasts, I do not have any preconceived notions or preconceived ideas, or questions coming at me in advance. We decide the topic based on the person who's asking the questions. They pick the topic and then we go from there, following the Spirit.

It's kind of exciting. I always like doing these because I find that I get more clarity and more understanding. It solidifies my testimony, and I learn a little bit more about what my mission is along the way. Joel, I'm gonna turn the time over to you. Go ahead and ask your first question.

Joel: I wanted to start in Alaska and work our way down. So if you could start just by talking about some of what you see happening up there in Alaska, and then maybe just kind of wander our way down to the continental United States.

Julie: I'll do that. We'll throw in the west coast of Canada, British Columbia, Vancouver, going into Seattle and over to Boise. We'll also talk about Oregon.

Let's start with that. Thanks for that question. I've had a lot of people actually email me and ask me about what I see for Alaska and Hawaii. I didn't travel to either of those states when I was doing my speaking engagements and didn't really discuss those regions.

Alaska, as you know, is the largest state in the United States of America. A lot of people forget about Alaska because they're isolated and separated, but I see an invasion there from the Russians. In fact, they have ports in areas that are near Alaska and they will try to take over Alaska, essentially.

I also see several very big earthquakes in Alaska that will cause large waves, and some of the land will be broken off. There will be crevices and other deep areas created in that part of the continent.

A lot of people from Alaska will be coming over into Canada as they flee some of those natural disasters and the foreign troops. Many people go into the mountains there, just like they will go into the mountains in other places in the world.

Due to the cold weather, the extreme conditions seem to be more extreme as natural disasters take place. There are actually some mountainous areas that will have volcanoes that will erupt.

They are gonna be greatly impacted and affected by these natural disasters, as well as war. On the coast of Alaska there will be Russian ships. The Chinese will come in there as well.

They'll also come into the Vancouver, British Columbia area. Already they have taken hold on that island. If you go into the center of Vancouver Island, you see that there is a large population of Chinese immigrants. They have come in and they are buying up land like crazy in that part of Canada.

That's basically what I see for that part of Alaska and Canada. Let's go over into Edmonton and Calgary, Alberta and also over to Cardston. Cardston is a place of safety, and it will become what we call a City of Light.

Cardston has a beautiful LDS temple there. It will serve as protection for some of the Saints. Other groups of Saints will come on down doing missionary work and rescue missions into the United States, and the other way around. Some of our members of the United States will go into the Cardston area to do rescue missions as well.

I'll now focus on the states of Washington and Oregon. I see a mass exodus of people going west into the Boise area and on over into other parts of Idaho, like Twin Falls, and the Rexburg area. Those people that do not flee or gather early on regret it due to natural disasters.

I see everything from Mount St. Helens and Mount Rainier erupting, and the foreign troops coming in as we go to war. I see thousands of people fleeing on foot, sometimes barefoot and with only the clothes on their back, or with only a small backpack or nothing at all. I see parents with children on their backs, similar to what is referred to in the Scriptures when you read about people in the Last Days and Tribulations fleeing with nothing on their backs.

That is the visual I get time and time again, especially for the states of Washington and Oregon. In respect to that, the Greater

Tomorrow Relief Fund is preparing places in the Boise area and other places in Idaho, specifically the Rexburg area, for these refugees.

These visions that I've had of just the state of Washington alone have caused me such sorrow and anguish and anxiety over the years that I'm very motivated to provide several safe houses. It is in the Ashton, Idaho, and Rexburg area where we're actively working, because I see not only thousands but eventually about a million people in that valley, coming from everywhere—Wyoming, Washington, Oregon, the Wasatch Front area of Utah—all coming up to the greater Rexburg area.

Oregon will be much the same as Washington. Portland and Seattle will be inundated with plague. The vials that I talk about in my books and the gallon-sized containers of biological weapons will be released in both Portland and Seattle. These are two of the cities that will have those vials poured in, particularly Seattle being the main one that it will spread from into the rest of the United States. The same goes for Salt Lake. We'll talk a little bit more about that, but Salt Lake is another place that I've seen inundated with that same gallon-size container.

I see tsunamis affecting both of those states. The Ring of Fire will come alive, affecting Washington, Oregon, and California significantly on a mass scale, so that parts of those coastlines are completely deteriorated, ripped off and separated from the rest of the continent. Does that spur any other questions about things that you might be interested in learning about that area?

Joel: No, I think that's a pretty good description of what will happen. Why don't we just keep moving down the coast to northern California, then southern California.

Julie: Okay, northern California. I see there will be Russian troops that will come into northern California in the Sacramento area, but they will essentially divide up, with some going as far south as San Francisco.

I see thousands of missiles being launched from the ocean, and they'll have missiles coming into the mainland of the United States from the oceans and from air. I see angelic forces as well as our own forces fighting against those missiles and other types of bombs, including nuclear bombs that are being let off in some of those larger cities.

Although it's mass chaos, what most people don't realize is how much angelic intervention is at our disposal. The damage is not going to be nearly as much as it would have been had all of them actually gone off. I see most of those missiles actually being detonated or the bombs being detonated, but then in some cases, due to Priesthood power, they're redirected back out into the ocean instead of hitting the land.

Make no mistake, the damage is extensive, but not nearly what it would have been had there not been divine intervention from the Light side.

This is going to be a massive war on the land, the sea, and in the air, and also on a spiritual level. The warfare that increases as the Tribulations begin and the portals of dark and the Portals of Light open up.

When our men and women are fighting against the invasion troops, they won't realize most of the time of what's going on in the Spirit World and how much protection they are given. So we don't lose nearly as many of our troops as we would otherwise.

Also, the whole goal of the Russians and the Chinese is to take our land without totally ruining the infrastructure. They want to enslave us and take over the land and everything that is of value, so they don't wanna totally destroy America. They wanna do the least amount of damage possible but get rid of the infrastructure so that they can build their own.

So they will use tactics such as EMP's. I do see an EMP affecting the United States and Canada, with concentrated efforts in the large cities. The EMP will cause complete blackouts for a period of time that I am not allowed to disclose. But it is long enough that you need to be willing and able to live for about a year without electricity, if not longer. In some areas it won't be that long. In some areas it will be a matter of days or months.

Some areas they don't ever get their electricity back, but that provides later on, clean clear circuits that have been blown where we can then utilize pure energy. That is something being developed as we speak. Pure energy that will be brought back to us. We can take those EMP'd circuits and start from scratch with clean, clear Light energy.

Returning to the coast of California, Sacramento and San Francisco will be inundated with plague and also tsunamis. The foreign troops keep coming in on a mass scale, mostly the Russians coming into Sacramento, and the Chinese and the Russians actually kind of fighting over San Francisco, because that's such a big city of significance.

I see Sacramento having earthquakes and volcanos. San Francisco will not only be inundated by Plague on a massive scale, but that city is hit harder than some of the other cities in the United States because a cleansing has to take place there. Because of that, the entire coastline appears to be ripped from the mainland because the tsunami does so much damage that it covers a large portion of the earth on that coastline.

We'll see an increase in dangerous waters, including an increase in sea life that comes ashore, including the great white sharks. Volcanoes will come alive that have been dormant, and we see both fractures in the earth and under the sea.

There are LDS temples in these regions. I have been given a visual of the LDS Oakland Temple. It survives these destructions, but it is essentially sitting on top of an island. So anyone that knows the topography out there, if you're thinking about staying in San Francisco, I hope you're a good swimmer.

When this huge tsunami comes in, it will flood much of that area out there. I see those San Francisco streets that are so hilly being flooded by the tsunami. Then as the water recedes, the tops of the streets in some areas are above water, but it makes it even worse, because the water just sits and has nowhere to go and it just stays there. Shops and businesses are completely destroyed. I need to take a break. You have any questions on that? That's a lot, right there.

Joel: (laughs) That is a lot. I think it's interesting that essentially what's happening as the troops come in is a polarizing effect where you either feel a pull to the Light, and it helps you come closer to God, or you feel a pull towards the darkness. Essentially, there will be no more fence sitters.

Julie: That's absolutely correct. That's how I see it as well. San Francisco's a good city to use for that example. There's a high population of Christians in San Francisco, and there's also a high population of people who've turned their hearts and minds and thoughts away from God. As a tender mercy from the Lord, He will cleanse that area.

I say "tender mercy" because He loves all His children. To keep them from further condemnation, He will simply wipe them from this Earth. He will end their mortal ministry and send them on to the other side of the veil to continue in their progression. They can continue to progress on the other side of the veil, whereas if they were to stay here in mortality, in their body, continuing to do some of the evil acts that they're doing, they will further condemn themselves.

So as an act of mercy, He removes them from the mortal body, away from the temptations and the entities that are plaguing them. He takes them to the other side so that they can continue in their progression. They will then have the choice as they go into the eternal spiritual realm to choose if they wanna go to the Light and accept Christ. They can choose if they want to continue on a Light path or if they want to continue in darkness.

Joel: I want to clarify what we mean when we say "Light" or "dark." When we get pulled toward the Light, we're actually becoming more selfless. To see somebody who has Light within them, the things they'll be doing is helping their neighbor, caring for others, and sharing what they have—the type of acts that Christ would do if He was on the Earth.

When we say "darkness" I think it's good to define that those kind of people will be greedy, wanting to steal from others and even kill people so that they have more. So when we say, "Light and dark," it's good to just say: "Listen, if we are Light, we are doing acts that help others and we are selfless."

Julie: I agree with you. Thank you Joel. I see, that brings me to the next point of what I see in every large city, with San Francisco again being an example. The plague will spread rapidly thanks to everything from lice to rats and mice. Other pestilence including ticks will spread the plague.

It will be as bad or worse than the days of the Black Plague in previous days. That actual plague will come back, as well as a myriad of other plagues. There's gonna be more than a handful of plagues that will be spreading.

They'll mutate. They've already scientifically developed these plagues in the lab. Some of them are spiritually created and have not yet been physically manifested, and others are physically manifested and created on the Earth already.

They've already taken some of the mice and rats and injected them, and they're waiting to release them into the public. They know that these animals mass produce. They've already released some of them, and that's why we have things like Ebola and other diseases are surfacing.

It is a lie that Ebola has been eradicated. They purposely injected people in Africa with the Ebola virus, and that is how they got it to begin with. That's obviously not something that is being reported. They have brought that to the United States. They're testing the waters on it. We don't hear about it because the media has been bought and sold by the Gadiantons, which is something we learn about in the Book of Mormon.

The term "Gadianton" describes a dark high-level operative,

everything from a high level conspiracist to anybody who is basically enlisted in Satan's cause. These Gadiantons have enlisted scientists, doctors, and politicians. They've enlisted just about everybody in their cause within every system of government, even within churches and communities.

They are conspiring to kill, destroy, hurt and injure innocent Americans and people around the globe. It is very wicked, it's very dirty, and it's been planned for decades, going back to 1913, when some of these government welfare programs were coming to fruition. That is how far back it's gone in the United States, and it continues to evolve with modern socialistic things involving George Soros and others.

That stuff is real, folks. Some of it sounds outlandish, some of it *is* outlandish, and some of the most outlandish stuff that's going on in the United States is absolutely true. When it comes to the plagues, there are ways that you can clear yourself of plagues. I've been learning some of that, but we won't take the time to go into that now.

If it's according to the Lord's Plan, you're gonna go to the other side of the veil. If it's not, you'll stay on Earth and God will make available a way for you to endure that plague.

It is something that we need to caution people about, and they need to be getting things in order in their homes. Not everyone will be able to go to places of safety in the middle of Idaho or Utah or New Mexico, or other places that are more isolated from large populations.

Most of the people in the United States will not be in a position to leave. They will be stuck in the cities, and that is where with mass concentrations we have more people on mass transit systems and other places where devastation can occur. We will have terrorist activities, marauders, and we'll have people who are interested in self aggrandizing.

Darkness will prevail in those cities for a time. That leads me into the topic that we're gonna do a podcast on that I'm excited about. We're gonna do a podcast based on rescue missions and the heroes that are gonna be in this country. I think that's gonna be a cool podcast.

Eric: Nice.

Joel: Yeah, that will be great. I think it's good to make a note right here. You've been talking a lot of chaos and things that will that will be happening that will cause people to have a lot of fear and anxiety.

It's important to remember that the author of that fear and anxiety is Satan. To help combat that evil, we really need to have peace in our lives.

Julie: Right.

Joel: Even in the midst of chaos, we need to have peace. We can produce that from within ourselves, with the help of the Lord. If you look at Christ's life, there was much chaos going on around Him, yet He was able to have peace. Through that peace and love that He had in His heart, He was able to overcome and escape a lot of things.

If we take that as our example, we can do the same things. Whether we're in San Francisco, or in Oregon, or wherever you're at, the Light side will be there to help you. The spirits that are good are out there to help, and if we can remain calm, it keeps Satan away from us.

In other words, keep away that anger and anxiety, and ask for that peace so that we can find strength to overcome many things. That's where people will find their power to overcome, to survive, and to help others.

Julie: Right. Thank you, Joel. I love that. I see darkness on the Earth, but I also see Light Portals opening up, and I see everything from angelic, translated, transfigured, and resurrected beings on this planet now coming in tenfold, preparing to help us when the

Tribulations do start. I have been privileged to meet some of these individuals. That might sound crazy, but that is the truth. I have met some of these individuals in real life, flesh and blood, talking to them, face-to-face. I am here to tell you that they're real, and they will help.

I've had a lot of angelic ministration. I have it every day. They remind me constantly that we are not alone. The Lord has a Plan, and if we have faith in His Plan, then we believe everything is for our good. Nothing is coincidental. Even the tragedies that occur in our lives and on this Earth will help us to become better, stronger, more noble men and women who can follow the Lord and build His Kingdom here and into the Eternities.

As we seek to glorify God, we are being able to increase in our understandings, increase in our power, and we increase in our knowledge and education. We can know about everything from spiritual warfare to what it's like to live in a spiritual realm and a physical realm that are unified and tied together. You cannot separate the two.

The more I go through difficulty, the more adversity I have, the more convinced I am of that. God is allowing me to learn what it's like to be like Him by suffering, by grieving, by expanding my knowledge and my sensory experiences. It absolutely is a beautiful Plan. It is a hard Plan, but it is worth it. I witness and testify it is worth it. We cannot give up in this fight against the adversary.

Joel: If we look at our Savior as our Exemplar, this is a part of the Plan. He overcame all things because He went through all things. If we are attempting to follow Christ, then it's only natural to look at that pattern and say, "All right then, what's next?"

What's next is that we go through these hard things, and we can overcome them as well.

There's no need to be scared. There's only the need to have faith, because truly believing in Christ is understanding that we *will* go through those things. It *is* a part of our Plan to do that, so we can progress and become more like Him.

Julie: I agree with you 100 percent, Joel. I wanted to add some more about what I see happening in northern California, because we talked for a minute about how people in the northwest will come into the Boise, Idaho area and on over, following the highways.

One of these days I think it would be good, Eric, if we could put some maps up and do a podcast where I can show people on the maps and we can outline what I see with where certain natural disasters will take place.

I'm not gonna be all-inclusive, because that's impossible to do. But I would love to be able to show people where some of those goods are that we're gonna store, so that people know where they can go for safety later on.

I'm not gonna give specifics because I don't want to let the enemy know where I've got my safe house, but I want to be able to give people a general idea of the regions involved and where I see those foreign troops coming in, and where they can avoid disaster, like on the main highways. For example, being careful on highway I-15, or some of those other main highways that come into the Wasatch Front.

In the northern California area I see mass exodus again, many people coming on foot. They'll start out in cars or motor vehicles. They'll run out of gas, the traffic will be too hard, or they'll get blocked off with security checkpoints. They'll also get blocked off from natural disasters, mudslides and other things.

They'll end up on foot, a lot of them, and coming through mountain passes or elsewhere through deserts and other discouraging circumstances. I see some of them coming from Nevada on over through the Virgin River Gorge into the St. George, Utah area. A large majority of the people coming from California and even Arizona will arrive in that area.

Another huge gathering place is north of St. George, with about a million people in that valley. I also see a huge influx of people into the Sanpete Valley, which includes Manti, Utah. There's also gonna be about a million people in that valley one day.

So there will be mass exodus from the Pacific coast and going inland. Imagine if you're living in that area and you're needing to help rescue people. There's going to be a huge need.

I ask that you go to my website: **www.julieroweprepare.com**. Learn more about the books that I have written, learn more about my mission with the Greater Tomorrow Relief Fund. Go into the Greater Tomorrow Relief Fund, check out the website **www. greatertomorrowfund.org** and you will see what our mission is.

If you have friends and family in that area I encourage you to donate money or to donate your time and resources. We are looking for safe houses in these cities and regions so that we can put supplies, we can stock up, and have things ready so when natural disasters start or the foreign troops come in, we can have safe houses for people who have been displaced.

We need your help, and we need volunteers. We are gonna be very selective in who our volunteers are. We do background checks on people and we will be very selective, especially with who I trust in these safe houses and with the confidential information.

We need to make sure that we have people who are of the Light who are going to share their supplies and their food, instead of hoarding it, and who can protect from marauders and other people. We have a system in place for that.

Okay, let's talk about southern California. Every time I'm shown this in vision, the first troops that land are the Russians in Seattle and Portland. Then the Chinese come, and they first hit the Los Angeles area, then San Francisco, then San Diego at about the same time.

But the first boots on the ground that I see are paratroopers, then the Chinese ships that come into Los Angeles. There are thousands of them. Thousands and thousands of them come into the Los Angeles area.

As you can imagine, with Los Angeles being the way that it is, and with how traffic is already, it's going to be nearly impossible at that time for people to get out of the area. They will be stuck there in transit because they will run out of gas.

You can see on the news when we've had Hurricane Katrina and other disasters, how hard it was for people to get gasoline. The lines were super long, they ran out of gas, the stores only took cash. So if you do not have emergency cash on hand, I encourage you to do so.

You should always have cash anyway. It's foolish if you do not have emergency cash. If you can only afford twenty bucks, keep twenty bucks in your wallet, in ones. But you need to have at least twenty bucks of cash on hand. Maybe you don't want to carry that much cash in your wallet because you're in a high crime area, but you want to keep cash where you can have access to it.

People have asked, "Should I get silver and gold?" Well, the dollar is gonna collapse, but you're gonna want cash. People will still take it for awhile. You're gonna need to have cash to be able to get gasoline, or bread, or water from the grocery stores at least for a few days, before they run out.

Within a matter of two to three days, the store shelves will be cleared out, and they won't be delivering gas to the gas pumps anymore. So I would be stocking up on at least a two or three week supply of food in your pantry with bread, water, and other necessities that you usually eat on a regular basis.

We're not talking about a year's supply or a 30-year supply of wheat or anything like that. I'm talking about what do you eat every day or every couple of days, that if the grocery stores were to go down and you had no way to go get groceries, that you could survive for at least two weeks. I would start there.

Joel: I think it's important to note that you really need to follow the Spirit. In other words, pray and ask Father, "What do I need specifically for my preparations for these things that may be coming?" For each person, it's gonna be something necessarily different. Not everybody is gonna have the same mission that they need to do to help provide for themselves and for others.

Julie: That's true, and we need people in place. If you were essentially foreordained to be in a certain city or location when this stuff takes place, then you don't go anywhere else. You stay where God tells you to stay. You help and serve. You do what you need to do, and have courage and faith to do that very thing.

I don't think there's any reason for us to be afraid or to be panicked about what's coming if we're doing everything we know that God wants us to do. Then we can endure whatever we need to.

I'm not afraid. I don't like what I see. I'm not *happy* about it. I used to be afraid, and I used to have severe anxiety. I'd wake up in a panic because I was being shown something that was so dark and so scary that it made me fearful, but I don't live in fear.

I have courage, and I have joy in my life and I am excited for when we get through this stuff, because the "greater tomorrow" is so good. Whether you're on this side of the veil or the other side of the veil, it is so good. You will never regret being in the right place at the right time, doing the right things. I testify of that.

It is so joyful, so happy, and so Light, that you are gonna wanna be a part of that. You're going to want to work as hard as you can to get there, especially if you're on Earth and you make it through these tribulations. It will be worth *everything* you've gone through.

Joel: I agree with that. We really need to understand and know in our hearts the message of Jesus Christ, because essentially that's what it is. If you want to boil it down, all of these things that we're talking about are to help people understand that if they have fear and anxiety, that is coming from Satan. Recognize that, and ask the Lord to take it away. Ask Him for peace.

That is the way that you can combat Satan's armies and his fiery darts. His fiery darts are those negative emotions, that darkness that we feel. We can get rid of that simply by asking our Heavenly Father to remove it from us and to give us faith in Christ's message, so that we can overcome those fiery darts of the adversary.

That is the biggest battle, because once you overcome that darkness, fear, and anxiety, you can essentially have that faith to know everything you do is according to the Plan of our Heavenly

Father and Jesus Christ. As we do those things in faith, we will have confidence, and Light, and peace. That is a peace that cannot be given to you by anybody else.

It is our own, individual responsibility to seek the Lord and seek that peace. Nobody else can stand between you and the Lord and say, "Oh, here's some peace." It is individual. We can talk about it and we can share, but we can't give it to anybody else. We can only show them the way, and they have to accept that Light.

Julie: Right. Thank you. I've been accused of instilling fear by writing these books and talking about this message. But if you saw what I saw, you would do everything in your power to motivate people to get that peace.

I didn't create this, I'm not making this stuff up. I'm not that creative to be able to come up with these stories. I just know that I've been asked to help wake people up so that they can understand the condition upon which we find ourselves, so that they can turn to the Lord.

Turning to the Lord is what gives you the peace. Then you can go through anything. I've been through some hard things in my life, and the only thing that has healed my heart, kept me alive, and continued to motivate me to live is because I've turned to the Lord and I continue to turn to Him. He is absolutely the One True King. He is The Way. That is where you find rescue to your soul. Eric, do you have anything to say?

Eric: Sure. Thanks, Julie and Joel. Great comments and questions. The thing that's coming to my mind as you've talked about some of the events coming like earthquakes, volcanoes, foreign troops, and plague, is I keep going back to Isaiah. In several places in the Scriptures, Isaiah mentions words like flee, fled, and forsake.

I wanted to point out to those who like to read and tie these things to the Scriptures, that I can count right now on this piece of paper in front of me six or seven really good scriptures that talk about a great forsaking that will take place in the Last Days. If you look at that word "forsake," it means to basically turn your back on something and walk away from it.

I think Isaiah saw the things you're describing when he talks about people fleeing and forsaking, and their homes are left uninhabited.

I wanted to see if you had any insight on that. Do you think that is the appropriate scripture for the things that you've been talking about?

Julie: Yes. Both John the Revelator and Isaiah saw exactly what we're talking about. I know this because I have had interactions with them, I still have interactions with them. They have continued to tell me and remind me that I am on the Lord's mission in modern days, playing a role similar to those in their day when they were asked by the Lord to witness and testify of End of Days. That's not end of the world, but the end of days as we know it.

Isaiah saw exactly what we're talking about. He has written beautiful prose. It's difficult for some people to understand, because it requires that you have the Spirit if the Lord to decipher what he's talking about. He absolutely saw what we're talking about. Do you have a list of those scriptures you can read off for us?

Eric: Yeah, let me run through some.
Isaiah 26: 20-21
Isaiah 6:11-12
Isaiah 5:9
Jeremiah 2:15
Jeremiah 33:10.

For LDS audiences, Doctrine and Covenants 115: 6, and First Nephi 17:38. The list goes on. There's quite a few references to this idea of people fleeing, leaving, forsaking, and then later on in the Scriptures it talks quite a bit about those uninhabited cities and homes being inhabited once again, which is curious.

Julie: Right. They're gonna be inhabited by anyone from foreign troops to marauders but later on, re-inhabited by those very people who used to live in them. I have seen what happens to the house that I live in right now. There will come a point in time when I need to go to a place of safety that's not my current home. Then I will come back to it within seven to ten years after leaving my home. After the tribulations are over, I will be able to return to my current home and residence that I live in right now. That brings me great joy and comfort. Not everyone will be able to do that.

Many people will have to forsake their homes and all their belongings. They will have to live in poverty for a long time and maybe rebuild in a new location. Some people will actually be called upon to return to their homes and rebuild their cities after we've finished the war.

Thank you for those Scriptures. Those are great. I hope you'll look them up. I just wanted to make one more comment for the LDS audience. For those who do not believe yet in The Gathering or The Gathering Principle, I want to bring to your attention the very first book in the Book of Mormon where Nephi is talking about his goodly parents. His father Lehi had seen in a vision that the city of Jerusalem was going to be destroyed.

I have experienced dreams and visions seeing that Kansas City will be destroyed. I live about an hour south of there. The Lord has warned me that my family and I will need to leave prior to that destruction. Not all of Kansas City will be destroyed, but it will have plague, and it will have a lot of gangs and other troubles that come out into the suburbs. It will not be a safe place to live for a time.

I have a mission that's gonna require that I go west for a while before I come home. If you look at the story in the Book of Mormon with Lehi, he flees with his family and he leaves without much notice. He knew for a long time he was gonna leave, but those in the city did not know that he was leaving.

He did that purposefully. He fled at an hour when he could

leave without people noticing that he was taking off. I want to point out that Lehi was not the Prophet during that time. It was Jeremiah. I encourage our LDS listeners to go back and read your Bible.

This is not meant as a judgment on my part, but what the Spirit has been telling me is that I need to encourage our LDS members to get back to their Bibles. They might be good at reading the Book of Mormon, but many of you are not reading your Bibles and do not know your scriptures.

If you did, you would understand that Jeremiah was the Prophet who lived in Jerusalem at the time and Jeremiah was warning the people as well of their wickedness. He perished with his people. Jeremiah perished with his people, and that was his mission. Lehi was told to leave with his family, and they came to the Americas. I witness and testify of this truth.

I have seen it in both vision and in dream, and I have been shown it in my NDE's when I have experienced the Window of Heaven that's talked about in my book *A Greater Tomorrow.* Go to julieroweprepare.com check out the books that are on there, and you'll learn more about my story.

I've got a blog on there, and you can read some of the quotes that I've written, and go ahead down to the bottom of my home page, and click on The Greater Tomorrow Relief fund to learn more about the mission of The Gathering and preparing for when we have refugees coming through.

I hope that you'll volunteer, I hope that you'll listen to this message, and know that the Lord loves you, no matter where you find yourself and you can have rest in the Lord.

PODCAST 7

❧

WHAT I SEE IN SOUTHWESTERN U.S.

Julie Rowe: Welcome to the Julie Rowe Show. We have a great guest on the phone, my friend Joel, and we've got Eric on the phone as well. How are you today, Joel?

Joel: Great! Thank you for having me on.

Julie: Sure. We've already done one podcast with Joel. We started talking about what I see in the United States, and we're gonna pick up where we left off. Eric, how are you today?

Eric Smith: Doing great. The weather is beautiful today.

Julie: Yes, it's beautiful here in Kansas, too. Blue skies, just a few clouds, and nice and sunny at 81°.

Eric: Nice.

Julie: So I just wanted to welcome you guys, and welcome the audience by saying, "Thanks for listening."

Today we're gonna pick up where we left off with Joel in talking about what I see in the United States. So I'm gonna turn the time over to Joel to ask questions. We left off in southern California.

Joel: Yeah, we actually didn't talk about southern California too much, so I was hoping to get to that today. Also, maybe some about Hawaii, Arizona, New Mexico, and *maybe* Texas if we can get that much in today. We'll see.

Julie: Okay. If not, we can talk a little bit about Nevada too.

Joel: Oh, excellent. Yes, I forgot about poor Nevada.

Julie: And if those people in Utah are lucky, we might talk about St. George. We could do a whole podcast just on the greater St. George area. Let's see what we can do.

We'll pick up where we left off in California. I didn't mention everything as far as disasters, but just think about everything that could possibly happen as far as natural disasters go.

You're gonna see that all over the world, like mudslides because of excess rain, or lots of snow that melts and causes mudslides. There will be plenty of severe storms with lightning and thunder, and lots of tornadoes.

I wanted to mention that, because I don't want people to think that just because I don't mention it that it won't happen. I can see already people say, "She never said anything about an earthquake in such and such place."

For instance, I haven't talked much about earthquakes happening in Idaho, or other volcanoes, but they will happen there. We'll talk a little bit more about Idaho later.

So just because I don't say it, doesn't mean I haven't seen it. But I don't know if I've seen everything. They've shown me enough to give me an idea of some of the things that are gonna happen in certain areas.

I know basic geography, but I've never studied these maps. I don't get on the Internet and study the geography of the United States or of the world. This is all stuff that's just been shown to me in night vision, and then I have follow-up day visions that go along with it.

Back to northern California for a moment. I do see mudslides happening there. Also, we're gonna have mass amounts of flooding. Then in other areas where we have had flooding in the United States, we'll have droughts and famines. We're going to live through everything that's talked about in the Scriptures, in the seven years of Tribulation.

In southern California, we pick up with the foreign troops coming into the Los Angeles area and then moving north. They also come through by air as they parachute down onto the land. They also come in by submarine and boat.

We're talking about massive amounts of Chinese troops coming in that area. They also go south into San Diego. They try to cut people off who are trying to find food, clothing, and shelter from the storms and other disasters. The people in southern California are trying to escape the cities where later there are mass execution and other really dark things, as well as tsunamis and earthquakes.

People at first try to go by car, motor bike, or any kind of vehicle they can. I even saw people getting on their horses who were more isolated, but they didn't live quite far enough away from where troops were coming through. They were trying anything rather than have to leave by foot.

But the majority of people end up doing mass evacuations on foot because the highways are broken up. The backroads are more accessible for a while, but there are marauders and gangs around. The earthquakes damage the prisons in a lot of areas, and the guards abandon their posts, allowing the prisoners to get out.

There are a lot of reasons why it becomes dangerous for people in these Last Days as they try to hunker down and find safety. In San Diego, we have a huge influx of people coming in from Mexico. It's already getting pretty dangerous when it comes to the drug cartels. We see that going into Arizona, too.

Let's transfer over into Arizona. I see a mass exodus of people in California and Arizona going north, along with those coming in from Las Vegas. I see nuclear explosions in both Phoenix and Las Vegas, and also in some of the coastal cities. The Las Vegas Strip in particular is pretty much annihilated, so a mass exodus of individuals heads to the Saint George, Utah area. But the Virgin River Gorge will be inaccessible. The pass is cut off.

With GTRF, that's one of the locations we are seeking to have supplies ready to be distributed so when people come on foot, or by whatever means they can, we are ready with as many supplies as we can to help give aid. I see people from Arizona coming to southern Utah, as well as from different parts of Nevada, like Reno.

In the Phoenix area, I see people going and trying to find safety in the Snowflake area, and some of those upper high desert mountain ranges. They try to find refuge there. In the Tucson area I see some of them going to Mount Lemon and other nearby areas. I used to live out there. Joel, you used to live out there. You know Mount Lemmon, don't you?

Joel: I do.

Julie: Yeah. So it's not a big enough mountain for everybody in Tucson, is it?

Joel: No, not at all.

Julie: Right. I see a lot of people there, but the troops do get over to Mount Lemmon, because it only takes about an hour to get up Mount Lemmon.

So if I were in your shoes and you live in Tucson, I would not go to Mount Lemmon. Don't count on that area being a place of safety. If you have nowhere else to go, it's better than staying in your downtown South Tucson neighborhood,

The drug cartels have already come into Phoenix. The human trafficking problem in both Phoenix and the Tucson area is huge right now, and it will continue to increase exponentially.

The headquarters are actually on the West Coast and they'll

bring them to Tucson and Phoenix. That's the route that they do. They'll also bring people from New Mexico into Arizona.

One of the reasons that the Lord brings the tribulations is to try to limit the damage that's being done by those Satanists and those people that are working in the human trafficking and drug cartels.

I see the Temple of Baal being erected in different parts of the United States. They've already got a gateway in New York and in London. They also have smaller gateways throughout the United States that they've been building but haven't been made public.

I see those gateways and those portals, and their doorways being opened up. I see them taking passengers into train stations and on public trains. So I caution you that later on when you have somebody in the government or in the military try to convince you to get on a bus, train, or subway with the promise of food, don't do it. Even if they're threatening that they're gonna injure you or your family. I caution you greatly against that.

In contrast to that, I do see the LDS Church providing buses in Utah to help get people to Places of Safety. The Church will be the main forerunner of the denominations that will provide Places of Safety, but there will be other churches and communities that provide safe havens for people across the United States.

The remnant of the government that is left at that time is basically entirely run by the Gadiantons. Anybody who had any allegiance to the U.S. flag or to the Constitution will rise up against the foreign armies to defend the Constitution.

The Elders of Israel and others within the United States who are called upon to defend the Constitution will go to war against the United States' Gadiantons and those foreign invaders , many of which have been indoctrinated with hate speech against the United States. Let's see, I think I need to take a breather. That might be a lot for people already. What do you think?

Eric: You talk about all these events unfolding, and I'm not gonna ask you when those occur, but can you tell us the sequence of events? We've already talked about the Wasatch Wakeup and then about a year later we see a bigger earthquake take place. Can you tell us when this all begins?

Julie: I don't know exactly when this occurs, and I'm not given permission to discuss timelines and specifics on this podcast. My understanding is: I am forty-four, and I believe we'll be invaded by the foreign armies before I'm fifty.

I don't know exactly when it will be. At the earliest, we have sleeper cells throughout the United States. They are waiting for their cue. We could have an entire podcast on sleeper cells. I see this being a combustible situation.

Please tell me one more time what your question was, because my mind was already jumping ahead, wanting to talk about sleeper cells and things like that.

Eric: You started talking about southern California and invading troops. Is that before, during, or after the Big One?

Julie: I see the Wasatch Wakeup happen, and then I see the Ring of Fire coming alive. So one earthquake triggers the other earthquakes. They all kinda coincide, and there are many, one right after the other. It's hard to say exactly when the foreign troops come in, because it feels like they arrive almost at the time the Ring of Fire in California opens up.

The foreign armies come up Highway 191, they also come up through I-15. They come on I-70, I-80, and all of the main highways in the United States. Their goal is to take over the airports, the schools, the hospitals, government buildings, and take over main highways and put checkpoints up. They will attempt to corral the most people and infrastructure with the least amount of resistance.

When the Big One hits Utah—not the Wasatch Wakeup, but the Big One that is at least a 9.0 on the Richter scale—then the foreign troops come in after *that*. Well, they come in to California, and later into Utah. I see them coming in a peaceful manner first to help with some of the troubles in California and Utah.

However, they already have their sleeper cells here. They're really here to take over and to put the American people into subjection of their governments and of their military. I see it happening in such a quick manner from all sides.

It quickly turns to war in the Southern states and in California, because the people have an uprising when they start realizing that the Chinese who have come in aren't friendly. I guess you realize that when you have a foreign army coming to your door saying that you need to leave, because they're gonna take over your house.

I see them heading into the Boise area after they've already gone in to Portland and Seattle. As they move inland, Utah is one of the first states they hit.

They also know that the LDS Church has encouraged its members to have food storage for a long time, so they believe they can go to Utah and get food. They also wanna try to minimize how many members of the Church escape their clutches, because they don't want an uprising. So their goal is to keep the LDS Church members from starting an uprising against them.

That is something that's been prophesied for generations, and members of the LDS Church know that. They've been raised with the idea that the "Elders of Israel" will rise up against those who would do combat on U.S. soil.

That's been prophesied by Joseph Smith and other prophets of the LDS Church. So another reason why the foreign army goes to Utah is to keep the LDS Elders of Israel from rising up to defend the Constitution. Does that help? I just went off, didn't I? Wow!

Eric: (Laughs) Joel, did you have any questions?

Julie: I've had a lot in my head! This feels good to get this out! I've been wanting to talk about this for a while.

Joel: She definitely answered your question there, Eric. I just want to say that one of the things I noticed was that many schools are getting solar panels and are basically becoming self-sufficient. I could really see the grid going down and if you want power, you gotta go to a school. The school is where they'll basically have the ability to control the population.

Julie: Right. They will actually do lockdowns at the school. One of the first things they'll do is lockdowns so that people are not able to get their children. They will use that as a way to try to coerce men to join the wrong side. It will just be amazing at how many lies they tell. They will basically use fear tactics. They will tell everybody that they have to get the chip in order to get food, or to get their kids back.

Then they'll say they need to chip the kids so that you can keep track of them, because it becomes so dangerous that if you don't chip your kids, somebody will steal them and put them in a human trafficking ring.

They will use the chip to monitor and track people. They have tracking devices in those chips, just like when you chip your dogs. A lot of those chips will have tracking devices already built in, and if you try to escape, they will know who you are, what your identity is, along with the members of your family.

They'll use that information to try to get you to confess, or to give away where other people are, such as the Elders of Israel or some of the other denominations that are preparing militias. Their tactics are everything that was used in the First World War, the Second World War, and there are even war strategies used in the Bible that will be employed in this war. They will have perfected their ability to read body language and human nature. They will use all of those tactics as weaponry against us, and I'm talking both in the physical realm and in the supernatural realm.

Joel: Wow.

Julie: You are right about the solar panels. They do have an ulterior motive for that. They'll put them at the hospitals and nursing homes because they'll try to basically get rid of the sick people or the old people. They can put a lot of citizens in those buildings, and they'll do experiments on people. We're talking about some really rough stuff.

I'm gonna get blamed for invoking fear in people. That is not the motive that I have here. If you are listening to this, you should feel fear, because what they are planning is wicked. But you need to move from a place of fear to a place of faith.

Knowledge is power, and when you have knowledge of something, you can prepare for it. If you are angry when you hear this message, I would beg of you to take stock of your emotions. Are you angry at Julie Rowe because you think I'm a fear monger? Or are you angry because you feel powerless, and you have these emotions coming up?

Maybe you are asking, "How could God allow this to happen?" When you move from a place of fear to a place of Faith, you have power. God, in His Tender Mercy, has shown me and thousands of other people on this Planet that these things are true. I know that because I've had thousands of people email me telling me that they've had dreams and visions or other personal revelation of their own, not even anything to do with my message.

They have just come back as a witness to *me* that I speak the Truth and strengthened my testimony. I am not the only person who's seen this. Thousands of people who've contacted me have been shown in dream or vision, or through other forms of revelation, that this is bound to happen in the United States.

Eric: Thanks for that witness, Julie. Should we steer things back to the geography? Joel, do you remember where we were in the geography?

Joel: Yeah, she had talked about Nevada and southern California, and now Arizona. So moving on to New Mexico.

Julie: New Mexico is a transition state. I see people coming in from Mexico, and coming in from the Gulf. They'll enter Texas and move westward, up through New Mexico. There are some mountainous areas where people can hide, so add those to the safe locations. We will have some safe houses in New Mexico, but study where the drug cartels are going right now. Pay attention to the back roads. The forces that come at us will be mostly utilizing the main roadways.

If it's not a natural disaster that breaks up the roadway, it'll be foreign troops or other checkpoints blocking off the highways. So we'll be utilizing the back roads, sometimes only being able to get there on horseback or by foot.

New Mexico is key, because we have people coming from the East Coast who are going to want access to the west's mountainous regions. Foreign troops coming from the east coast will be blocked off by our troops. They'll also be blocked off when the Madrid earthquake happens. Some of the foreign armies that come into the East Coast will be drowned in that inland ocean that's created by the Madrid earthquake.

So I see people coming up through Texas, going through New Mexico and then into southern Utah through the Monticello area going up Highway 191.

I see people coming from the Kansas City area going south down through Oklahoma and then taking the same route through New Mexico on the way to southern Utah because the Denver area becomes so dangerous.

It will be really hard to travel through Colorado. The mountain passes in Vail and some of those areas will either be blocked off or they get blown up when the troops have taken over. They will blow them up , and in some cases we will blow them too.

So there will be a lot of different ways that Colorado is blocked off from the rest of the West. I-80 going through Wyoming is going to be very difficult and dangerous as well. The headquarters of the UN and the foreign troops will be at the Denver Airport. That is not just a conspiracy. They are already doing things at the airport. They are planning for mass executions, they're planning for a mass takeover. They they have reasons. If you were to look at the topography of the United States and the location of Denver, you can see exactly why they would wanna make that their headquarters.

When D.C. is destroyed, the President will try to make his way from Washington D.C. They do have safe tunnels they developed for members of the Government. Those are real, they're not just rumors. They do have very dark plans for some of those leaders to be safely hidden away. They have food supplies stocked away, and they are planning to leave the American people completely unprotected.

Joel: Wow. That takes care of Colorado and New Mexico, and a little bit of Texas.

Julie: For Colorado we also have Fort Carson near Colorado Springs, Colorado. That's a beautiful military installation with some of the highest technology and the highest military intelligence. That area also will be taken over by the dark forces.

There's a highway there, I-25. They will block it off and have checkpoints there. It actually will be impossible to go from Colorado Springs to Denver. The same with Fort Collins.

There's a reason they have put in all of those toll booths. Wherever you see toll booths in the United States, for the most part, those will be transitioned into checkpoint locations so that they can stop vehicles. They will search the cars, abscond people and supplies, then take food and other things so that they can use it for their benefit. Think about how many toll booths they're putting in just around the Denver airport. In the Denver area they have grown exponentially in the last five years.

Eric, do you have anything else that you wanted to say?

Eric: Well, I keep thinking about some Scriptures, as you talk about these people moving around. Foreign troops and disasters create this movement of people. I'm asking myself: "Who is moving? Is it the righteous? Is it the wicked?"

A number of Scriptures come to mind. Revelation 18:4 says: "And I heard another voice from Heaven saying: come out of her my people that ye be not partakers of her sins and that ye receive not of her plagues."

So I'm thinking, who's moving? It's the righteous people who are leaving the wicked. Isn't that right?

Julie: That is correct. In some cases, it is the righteous fleeing the wicked areas and the wickedness that surrounds them, for their very lives.

Eric: I think a lot of times when we read these Scriptures we've gotten in a habit in our culture of thinking of it as a Spiritual thing, you know, "Come out of Babylon."

We say, "Don't shop on Sundays and don't partake of Babylon's evils," but I wonder if these ancient prophets and John the Revelator meant that as a literal thing. "Come out," like, *leave.*

Julie: That is my understanding. I was shown much of what John was shown, much of what Alma in the Book of Mormon and Lamoni was shown, and even Moses and some of the others. They have communicated with me that this is a literal gathering in a physical sense: a coming out of Babylon.

We need to be ready to move if the Spirit tells us to move. In some cases it means we need to move into our yard because there's a group of women and children that need our house. Or we're a man and we need to give up our bed because there are orphans or women that have come on foot.

We need to be able to move and sleep in a tent in our front yard. In other cases it means we better be ready to move if we wanna be protected spiritually or temporally. That means we might have to move clear across the United States.

So when the Spirit speaks to you, listen. Whether that's because you know in the next month you need to go somewhere because the Spirit has said: "Hey, you need to get a job in Texas, instead of the job that you have in Arizona." Or if you need to move from Florida over to Kansas, or from Kansas over to Idaho, you go when the Spirit tells you to go.

That should be no different than what we do in our normal lives, but unfortunately many of us are very rusty on learning how to listen to the Spirit and act on it quickly.

All right. We're gonna wrap it up. Joel and Eric, thank you so much for your time today. I think this has been a good show, and hopefully it's been informative for people. Thanks guys for your time. I appreciate all you do.

PODCAST 8

THE GATHERING AND GTRF

Julie: Hi, we'd like to welcome you to the Julie Rowe Show today. Today I have my friend Keith on the line, and my friend Eric. We're gonna go ahead and start with Keith introducing the topic today that he has chosen. How are you today, Keith?

Keith: I'm great. Thanks for the invitation to do a podcast with you.

Julie: Thanks. Hi Eric!

Eric Smith: Hey, how's it going?

Julie: Good, thanks for helping us with this again today. Okay, we're gonna turn the time over to you, Keith, to introduce the topic for us.

Keith: Julie, in your books and radio interviews, you talk about Tribulations and calamities that are coming soon. You also talk about a Gathering, sometime after the Wasatch Wakeup earthquake, but before these Tribulations get really bad.

This concept of gathering is one that is seen many times throughout Scripture, and in history. One of the most well-known events is the Lord gathering the Children of Israel out of the land of Egypt. So is this Gathering you have seen a physical gathering like that?

Julie: Yes it is. It's absolutely a physical gathering. I actually see some of The Gathering beginning already. But the main impetus for the Gathering happens after, like you mentioned, the Wasatch earthquake, which is a 6.6 to 7.0 earthquake centered in the epicenter of University of Utah in Salt Lake City.

That kind of sends us into the Tribulations, or what they call the Days of Sorrow that's talked about in the Scriptures, specifically in Isaiah and the Book of Revelation. So that Gathering is a physical Gathering that happens throughout the United States, and throughout the world.

Keith: Will this happen all at the same time?

Julie: No, it doesn't happen all at the same time. I do see different denominations, different faiths and different groups and communities doing their own gathering. One of the main gatherings I see—and it impacts me and my family because I am of the LDS faith—is the LDS Church gathering members of their Church, and those outside of the Church that are able and willing and wanting to go, to Places of Safety.

That gathering has been prophesied in books of Scripture and by both modern and ancient-day prophets. I see that event being one of the gatherings that affects many of the people in the western United States, in the Intermountain area.

Keith: Yeah, I've seen some people already that have been moved upon by the Spirit of the Lord to move and change their physical location. So will some of those individuals that maybe have already made a move end up in the same place that the large groups do? Will they end up together?

Julie: Yes and no. I see families and communities gathering together. I see many people gathering in the LDS faith in their wards and stakes after an initial call to gather from the Prophet of the LDS Church.

It's not a commandment. It's an invitation for members to Gather together to find places of safety. I see that coming from the First Presidency of the Church, and then it filters down through either letters and/or broadcasts to the church buildings through satellite systems.

Members of the Church are then gathered together, and the Saints have the opportunity to travel to different locations, such as Girls Camps and other places that have been set up by the LDS Church in preparation for the Days of Tribulation.

Eric: I've been thinking about the Syrian refugees and the movements going on in Europe. While it's not exactly spiritual, or doesn't seem to be, do you see that as part of a gathering?

Julie: I see a lot of movement of people throughout the world as part of The Gathering. It's been talked about in Scripture for a long time that in the Last Days, prior to the Lord's Second Coming, that we will be gathered together as a people.

The Lord loves all of His children, so I do see gatherings taking place, with people coming out from their current locations and going to Places of Safety to find refuge. There will be many opportunities for people to learn about Christianity.

So once their physical life is sustained, it effects their spiritual life as well. It's a layered topic. I see this going on also in the Eternities as well, as the Lord is gathering His children on the other side of the veil in preparation for the Final Battle, prior to the Lord's Second Coming.

It's hard to just pinpoint one specific time or location for The Gathering, because this is a big Earth and this is a big Universe. But in talking about The Gathering in the physical sense, there will be movement of those in the Middle East areas. The Children of Israel, specifically the House of Judah, have been returning to Jerusalem and other parts of Israel for several years now, and that has been prophesied of for a long time as well.

Eric: I have a dear friend who's a Lutheran. I was asking her if her Faith has any plans of gathering, and she says they do. They don't talk about it a lot, but they have food stored, and they have a plan in place, so it seems broader than the LDS faith. I'm glad to hear that there are other Christians who are interested in this idea too.

Julie: Right. The LDS Church in particular has encouraged members of their faith to reach out in their communities. Members have been encouraged to provide food and other life-sustaining supplies to refugees, and to help donate to refugee programs.

That's one of the reasons I started the Greater Tomorrow Relief Fund, or GTRF, in the fall of 2015. It is a non-denominational, non-profit 501(c)(3) organization. We work with faith all over the country with the goal to eventually expand globally.

Right now we're just in the United States, where I work with the Jewish community, the Episcopalians, the Catholics, the Pentecostals, a lot of the Born Agains, and the Baptists. Any group that believes in End Times, believes that there is something coming that will change America.

I am finding that as I reach out to these organizations, whether it be Catholic Charities, the Red Cross, and other 501(c)(3)'s, there is a common thread and desire, which is to save lives and give hope to those who are in need. The Gathering is the whole basis for my non-profit organization.

Keith: Since you mentioned GTRF, or the Greater Tomorrow Relief Fund, let's talk about that just a little bit more. Can you go into more detail of what that mission is? There are other existing church organizations and relief organizations out there, so why did you create GTRF? What is different about that?

Julie: I appreciate you asking that. I've had a lot of emails come in from people asking why I created this organization and what the purpose is. They basically want to know how GTRF is different from other organizations, and why should they donate to my organization?

I completely understand why people would have questions about it. I first saw this organization in vision several years ago. I woke up from my NDE and remembered that I was supposed to one day have warehouses of supplies and provide safe houses.

So I've known this since 2004, although I didn't know how it was going to come to fruition. I didn't quite understand and have a whole picture of what it would be. I still don't have a complete picture, other than I know that the Lord is connecting the dots for me as I meet more individuals who have their areas of specialty.

Many people have had the same inspiration and have started their own organizations, and who have been prepared specifically to contribute to this mission.

A large portion of my personal mission, and therefore the mission of GTRF, is that as we go into the Tribulations prior to the Second Coming of the Lord Jesus Christ, there will be a lot of movement of individuals who will be homeless due to natural disasters or civil unrest, or due to the arrival of foreign troops.

So the goal of GTRF is to save lives and to give hope. That is kind of our tagline. I have been shown where these huge movements of people will be going after the natural disasters and invasions, so that way we know where we're gonna need to put supplies. That is why we're building support teams in various regions of the United States. Again, this will end up going globally, but for right now we're just starting with the United States, because that's where I see the most imminent need.

As we have war come to the United States in the next few years, survival becomes absolutely critical and supplies will be limited. That's just a product of being in war. The Thirteen Month War will create everything from a high mortality rate and starvation. Going on at the same time we will have plagues and pestilence, along with the natural disasters. So in anticipation of that, I am networking with groups across the country to build supplies and to have safe houses and warehouses in other locations.

We will have water supplies and food on location, but we will also have shoes, clothing, and hygiene kits available. We will have ways to transport these items that will become absolutely critical to the survival of millions of people.

Keith: It sounds like there will be a huge need all over the place. How will you choose where to focus your efforts?

Julie: I've been told and shown through the Spirit where those individuals are gonna be coming from and where the majority of the safe houses and properties need to be located. In many cases, people are not going to be living in a safe house. They will be living in a tent, as a refugee. You already see that going on in Europe and other locations in the world. When there has been a natural disaster, that is what happens—tent cities. So we are buying and stocking tents, and we're buying hygiene kit supplies.

We're looking for individuals that I can trust, that I know personally, that are willing to take refugees in. We'll be creating maps to those locations, and we have been developing interfaith networks to be able to communicate on everything from human trafficking needs to the basic survival needs of people coming through on their own.

So it's a layered effort and a very complicated thing that I'm trying to take on. But the Lord has been putting people in my path and it's absolutely magnificent to work with some of the most amazing people I've ever met in my life. They have such good hearts, and they are such good, giving people that have been specifically prepared to take part in The Gathering effort.

Keith: How does someone get involved with GTRF if they're interested?

Julie: You can go to my personal website, which is: **www. julieroweprepare.com**, and on my homepage you can scroll down to a link to the Greater Tomorrow Relief Fund's website. That's the easiest way to do it.

If people just wanna Google my name and then go to my website, then they don't have to necessarily remember the website for GTRF because there is already a counterfeit website. I've actually seen the counterfeit website. It is a non-profit, but it is not mine. I believe it's tied to a government entity. After I went public with mine, that site showed up, and I don't want people thinking that is mine.

There have also been some fake YouTube videos and other things that I saw this week now that my podcasts are up. So just be aware that there are people who are posing as The Greater Tomorrow Relief Fund.

If you're trying to find mine, make sure it has the background of a mountain scene and my picture on it. I only have *one* GTRF website and it is: **www.greatertomorrowfund.org.**

There's a volunteer button you can click on, and there's a donate button there. If you go to the volunteer page, it asks just basic information, and then we have members of our team that will get back to you. I will get back to you personally if I have a need for an area specialist in your region.

We have our division coordinators, regional coordinators, and area coordinators that have already been selected, but I am still looking for quite a few volunteers that can help as "boots on the ground." These people would be able to make hygiene kits and to get education materials ready for kids, because it'll be necessary to homeschool children and things like that.

Keith: You have mentioned before some of the things that volunteers might be doing in the future for GTRF, such as rescue missions. Are there some examples that you could share of what you see might be happening?

Julie: Yes, I can. I see about a million people in the greater Rexburg Valley, and also about a million people in the Sanpete Valley that includes Manti, Utah. I also see about a million people in the St. George Valley. Those are some of the locations that I want up on the radar for people. These areas will be considered more safe than some of the areas.

There are a lot of places in the country that are gonna be more dangerous, and some that will be more safe than others. I'm doing a lot of concentrated effort in those safer locations just because I see the mass numbers of exodus of people going there. But we will have safe houses positioned throughout the country for people as they make their journeys.

You can imagine if you have troops from a foreign army coming in and hitting everything with missiles and paratroopers landing. There will be major chaos.

Just think about the demographics and the geography of the United States. If we were at war in this country, where would the areas of vulnerability be? Most water sources will be tapped or controlled by the invading armies. We will be dealing with water shortages and contamination, as well as food shortages.

So being as self-reliant as possible is the first step. Second, be willing to share with your neighbors, so that you can join together as a unified group to combat somebody that might come to your home that is an unfriendly force.

Keith: You mentioned some of these places that will be safer places. Where is a safe place to consider?

Julie: Well, ultimately I need to emphasize that the true safety comes through relying upon the Holy Spirit and relying upon the Lord to get direction for where you need to go and what you need to do with your family. First and foremost, your relationship with the Lord is the most important thing.

It doesn't matter how much food or clothing or water or other supplies you have. If your relationship with the Lord is not where it needs to be, you cannot receive divine guidance and inspiration to know where to go for safety.

That's gonna be a play-by-play scenario for each individual and family, because there's simply not enough girls camps, church camps, or tent cities to be able to house everyone in the United States.

It may be that your family is meant to hunker down in a certain location and be there for someone else who might need your help. So in saying that, we don't want everyone fleeing to Rexburg Idaho, or Manti Utah, or to St. George. You don't wanna go prematurely. You go when the Spirit guides you to go. If you feel like you're supposed to take a job somewhere, for instance, you do that. People are being gathered all the time.

There are a lot of people in the Kansas City area that have gathered here. It has been because they got a job, or they're going to dental school, or another reason that they're living here that makes complete logical sense. But the Lord has a higher purpose in having them here in this region at this time.

There are places I wouldn't go, later on, but they're perfectly safe to live there now. So I don't want to invoke fear, or in any way influence someone's decision. That needs to be an individual choice that people make.

Rely upon prayer and Scripture reading, and listen to those who are in authority in the LDS Church that can give counsel. But recognize that we don't wait to be acted upon. We take action, and we are a proactive and a self-reliant people.

The Lord does not command in all things, and He expects us to use our discernment and to use the gifts He's given us to be proactive in our understanding of what He'd have us do.

Eric: It kind of feels like you're saying that if you're following the Spirit and living the Gospel, in all likelihood you're probably already doing what you should be doing, and you are where you should be at this time.

Julie: That's exactly how I view it. Right now my family and I live about an hour south of Kansas City, and we live in a rural location. That's where the Lord wants me to be. There are purposes for that. This property will be a way station where we can provide for families that are gonna come through when they have need.

Right now, there's just my family here. My husband has his job and I work from home. It is a situation that's not any more different than our neighbors on either side of us. We go to Kansas City all the time, and we lived up there for almost eleven years, but this rural location is where the Lord wants us.

There are higher purposes for why he wants us here now, but there will come a time when I won't be living here. I've seen that I will be going west to help the fulfill my mission in other ways, but some of my friends stay in the Kansas City area, and that's exactly where they're supposed to be.

Other people will be in Texas and Pennsylvania, and that's exactly where they're supposed to be. Key people will be in different places all over the country.

It isn't for me to tell somebody where they need to go. I'm just supposed to share what I know, testifying as a witness of God's plan, and let you know that you don't need to be afraid of anything you do, as long as you have the Lord on your side.

Keith: Sometimes it seems like a physical gathering is the focus the discussion. But you mentioned the Spiritual Gathering that is also taking place. What does that Spiritual Gathering look like?

Julie: Well, there's a Spiritual Gathering on both sides of the veil that I see going on. There's a lot of anxiety in people right now on this side of the veil, and actually on the other side of the veil there's some anxiety too, because they are preparing just like us.

They are preparing their troops on the other side of the veil to come and help with angelic ministrations. They will also help with The Gathering, and as we go to war.

When we going into the Tribulations, not only is it physical warfare on Earth, it is spiritual warfare like we haven't seen on the planet. So those on the other side of the veil are preparing their troops to go to battle, with the Light side against the dark side.

Both sides are preparing. I see mass numbers of entities that are lining up in certain parts of the country in preparation for battle on a spiritual front. Thankfully, the Light side is light years ahead, so to speak, in being able to combat the dark energy that will be upon the earth.

It is all being orchestrated by God, for a higher purpose, which is to bring us home to Him. We are learning what we need to do to become more like Him, and it's really a beautiful thing.

The orchestration is absolutely fascinating to me, because although I don't see all of it, every once in awhile I get a glimpse at what's going on just with the work that I'm involved in. I think it's magnificent that through Ministering Angels the Lord can accomplish so many great things in guiding us through the Holy Spirit.

He may send a relative to you that you don't even know is around you to guard you as a Ministering Angel. That relatives responsibility is not only to guard you, but to guide you.

You might have impressions that you need to run a certain errand, for instance. While you're running that errand, you run into a friend and you have a conversation that leads to something else, like a job interview. Or maybe it will lead to some kind of activity that you're supposed to be involved in the community.

The orchestration is absolutely fascinating. I'm just continually amazed at God's Tender Mercies and His love and ability to guide each of His children on the path that they need, individually and collectively.

Keith: Thanks. The idea of the physical Gathering takes a spiritual decision too.

Julie: It does.

Keith: The idea that the Prophet invites us to physically leave is interesting to me, because that is the first story in the Book of Mormon. Lehi receives a dream to gather his family and a few of his physical possessions such as his tents and food storage. Then they leave most of his worldly wealth and possessions behind, and gather out to a different physical location.

There's a spiritual gathering too. They go back to get gold plates as part of the spiritual preparation and work that happens there. But that's interesting to me that it is the first story in the Book of Mormon, and it happens over and over again.

Julie: Yes, in the Book of Mormon, the first story that is shared is read more than any other story in the Book of Mormon. Why? Because people continually say they're gonna read the Book of Mormon, and maybe they only get a few chapters in. But they read the story of Lehi, Nephi, Sam, Sariah, Laman and Lemuel—the family of Lehi—leaving and going into the desert.

That part of the book has been read more than any other book of Scripture in the Book of Mormon, and it was not coincidental. The Lord designed it that way, even though it is not written in chronological order.

What's the purpose behind it? Why the Lord would put that as the first book? Because He knew people would read that one the most. That's how important that story is.

The other reason it is included there is because when Lehi left Jerusalem, Jeremiah was the Prophet. Lehi was not the prophet when he had those dreams and visions and was commanded to leave. Lehi did try to get more people to leave. They had other friends and family, but from what I've been shown, they left family members behind that were unwilling to go.

They did not believe Lehi and thought he was just crazy. They felt he was just being kind of weird that he would wanna leave everything behind. So the others did not go. They didn't have the faith. They didn't believe him when he cautioned and warned them.

At the same time, Jeremiah was warning the people in Jerusalem. He was testifying and witnessing to them that if they did not repent, they would be destroyed. Jeremiah's mission was to stay with his people. Some of them later fled into the wilderness, but it was too late. Jeremiah actually perished during that time.

He was the actual Prophet of the Church at the time, not Lehi, and I think that's the pattern people need to pay attention to. We're being given warnings, and we are being given guidance and opportunities to learn about the things that are coming. We need to pay attention to those.

I am not the only voice out here. We've got Chad Daybell, and Hector Sosa, and several other people that are not of the LDS faith that have had NDE's.

I've had literally thousands of emails from people that live in all different parts of the United States. Some even live as far away as Australia, Europe, Canada, and South and Central America. They have emailed me that have heard about my story, and they have thanked me for sharing it, because they too have had dreams and visions.

Even if it was just one dream or one vision, they know I speak the truth and they have had an answer to their prayers that what they have been shown is actually, legitimately going to happen.

Keith: That is true, because I've talked to many people that have not spoken publicly or written a book that have had those same types of experiences. I see it over and over again.

Julie: Right.

Keith: Back to that first story that we mentioned of Lehi and Nephi and the Book Mormon. They invited others to go with them, but not very many go. What happens with this latter-day Gathering? Does the same thing happen? Do not a lot of people go?

Julie: Yes, very few will go. What happened to those who didn't go with Lehi? They either perished in Jerusalem, or they fled to other locations. Those that didn't go with Lehi and his family beforehand suffered greatly when the tribulations in those days started.

The people were left to flee on foot out of the city before Jerusalem was destroyed as well. Some of those groups broke off, but a large percentage of the individuals that did not listen to the Prophet were destroyed and went to the other side of the veil.

Keith: So looking forward, when there's a future invitation to gather by a Prophet, what happens to those that decide not to go this next time?

Julie: I see them going through torturous situations, either because someone gets hold of them or their loved ones. Many die a slow death of starvation, or they are subjected to severe atrocities. In some cases they end up fleeing afterwards, and then they get to a Place of Safety.

I see quite a few non-LDS people that didn't ever hear anything about this beforehand, but they come. I see a large number of individuals coming into the greater Rexburg area that are not of the LDS faith. They flee from other parts of the country.

The majority of those non-members that reach Rexburg are later converted to the Gospel. Many of them do not even believe in Christ at first, but many of them will end up having their testimonies strengthened. Their testimonies will begin to grow because they will be brought down to their knees, literally, in humility. So there are higher purposes, right?

Keith: Right.

Julie: I'm just doing the best I can to spread the word and to witness and testify, especially to members of the LDS faith, who I believe have a responsibility over our brothers and sisters. We are members of a congregation that covenants with God to serve others and consecrate all that we have. So that's why my voice goes to a lot of the people that I identify with, knowing some of these covenants we make.

It doesn't stress me out if someone doesn't believe me anymore. It doesn't stress me out if somebody isn't gonna listen to the Prophet, because I see things in more of an eternal perspective, and I believe so strongly in agency.

We don't wanna force our energy on someone. It's totally wrong to force someone to listen to a message, or to try to get them to see our way in a forceful manner. We testify to them—and I can be very bold in that—but I would never take someone's agency away. That is totally contrary to God's plan.

My hope is that people will listen and pay attention, then take it to the Lord and do whatever He tells them. Then they should trust that everybody gets their own answers, and they're on their own path and journey.

If they're supposed to go through hard things in Salt Lake City, or in Los Angeles, or in Phoenix, then I trust that the Lord is molding them into the individual that He knows they can become.

Keith: Thank you, Julie. One of the questions I had ties in with this. You created this Greater Tomorrow Relief Fund to help facilitate some of this Gathering. Your goal is to assist these people so that physical supplies would be there for them. Earlier we talked about donating to that fund, but you also have talked about the value of the dollar eventually becoming worthless. Could you talk about that again?

Julie: Sure. The dollar will collapse. Gold and silver and other commodities will be useful for a while on a bartering system. But there will come a point in time, not long after the dollar collapses, that none of that will even be valuable, because what's gonna matter is what's gonna keep someone alive. So a bartering system will be going on for quite a while.

We want to be ready before then, though. We're trying to get supplies in place now with the money that we have, while it's still good. I would just ask that you take this to the Lord. Ask Him what you need to do individually and for your family.

First and foremost, getting at least a two-week water supply and the two-week supply of food for your own family is crucial. Then get three months of rotatable goods. From there, if you have the money to be able to get a year's supply of food, like we've been counseled to do, then do that. But don't go into debt for it. There are people that have gone into debt for this, and that is not the Lord's plan. Have trust in His plan and get a little bit as you can.

When you have sufficient for your needs, then think about what to stock up on regarding supplies for somebody that might come to your own door. Then if you have excess, and it will not put your family in jeopardy financially, think about donating to a relief organization. Mine might be the right one, but there are so many good causes out there.

We do want to be charitable, and we want to be kind. If you feel that this message is resonating with you and you feel like helping with The Gathering, then seriously consider donating whatever amount you can. Five dollars can pay for a hygiene kit for someone. If you'd rather donate supplies, we do have some ability to take supplies. But donated funds make it easier for us to buy things on location. You know, we don't want used underwear or used socks.

There will come a point in time where people in their communities will use that kind of stuff, but initially from a hygienic standpoint, we're gonna be buying new socks and underwear. That's what we've been doing.

I haven't been instructed by the Spirit to engage people in collecting items like a Goodwill or a Deseret Industries and separating those items out. We already have Goodwills and D.I.'s. That is not the purpose of GTRF. What I'm looking at is if someone donated $500, what can I do with the $500 that will be the most beneficial for our mission?

For example, we're buying toothpaste in bulk, so that when we have 50 different families come to a safe house, we have toothpaste we can give them. The same goes with combs or brushes, or socks and underwear.

As far as any other used clothing, we are getting close enough to the Tribulations that if your children have outgrown those clothes, and you're in a place where you think you're going to stay, then I would encourage you to hang onto them. That way when people come to your door, you can give a pair of shoes to a toddler or a coat to somebody that doesn't have one. There are so many different ways that we can help.

As far as actually donating to GTRF, you can, you can mail a money order. I don't want to do regular checks because that gets difficult. So if you do a money order or cashier's check, you save the receipt for that, that's a tax write-off on the 501(c)(3) nonprofit. You have it written out to GTRF, or The Greater Tomorrow Relief Fund, and you can send that to my mailing address for GTRF at P.O. Box 895, Ottawa, Kansas, 66067.

That address is just for monetary donations. Please don't send supplies unless you email me first, because we may want to send those to Idaho, California, or Utah where we are better equipped to store them. I also don't want the post office to be inundated with boxes of shoes and things that I don't anticipate.

Keith: When you talk to many people, they say: "Boy, this sounds like a lot of doom and gloom."

Is there anything good about this Gathering and future events, to look forward to? Is it something besides just doom and gloom?

Julie: I'm glad you asked that. I love my life. I love where I live, I love my family, and I love the many blessings that I have. But I do look forward to the day that the Savior will return and this dark energy on our Planet will be eradicated. That is the Greater Tomorrow that I see. That is when we can be gathered home as beloved sons and daughters of a Father in Heaven that really loves us. He misses us and wants us to be happy and be like Him.

However, we can have a greater tomorrow, today. We don't have to wait. Where we are now, very much sets the stage for where we'll be tomorrow and in the coming years. Focus on the things that make us happy and that are of real value, like spending time with our friends and family that uplift us. Spend time on meditation and other spiritual things that help us gain peace in our hearts so that we can have a greater tomorrow, today.

Then we can be ready for the *real* Greater Tomorrow, and to be in the right place at the right time to accomplish the Lord's designs.

Keith: Thanks. I know that there's gonna be some great things that occur in the future, including miracles and rescue missions. It looks like a great and joyful time to be here on Earth. The difficult times are short, and won't last a long time.

Julie: Right. Look at the history of this Earth. When we've been at war and had other difficulties throughout the generations of time, some of the greatest heroes have arisen during those tribulations. Some of the greatest figures that have ever been on this planet came about in the times that were of most difficulty. I think we're gonna see a lot of heroes that are gonna rise up out of this, and they're gonna be better for it.

When I say heroes, I think of everyone from people who are progressing in their eternal progression here and on the other side of the veil. Heroes who are saving lives and giving hope and encouragement. They are finding rest in their soul because they are doing exactly what they were made to do, which was to find out what their true identity is and follow the Lord.

That way they find peace, they find satisfaction, they find health, healing, and help, and they become better people because they were meant to do this.

They were foreordained to come forth in the latter days to accomplish the Lord's designs and in so doing, accomplishing great things for their personal growth as they advance on their progression on the eternal round.

Keith: I think it would be fun to do a podcast on some of these future miracles and things that are gonna take place. It's an exciting time to live and be a part of, and I'm looking forward to it.

Julie: Thank you. I appreciate that idea, I think that would be terrific to talk about some of what I see with miracles within and without the camps, within different societies and regions of the country, and different parts of the world. Then we could talk on a broader scale about rescue missions as they are tied to missionary work and other things. I think it's a magnificent idea.

Keith: That sounds good. Is there anything else about a physical gathering or a spiritual gathering to add?

Julie: I just wanna encourage people to study their Scriptures and look at the patterns in the Scriptures that are there in the Book of Mormon, the Bible, and the Doctrine and Covenants. The patterns that we have discussed are there.

Those who are having trouble accepting this as part of the doctrine, I witness and testify to you that I am speaking the truth. I'm not here to try to convince you because I have anything to gain of my own. I'm here to tell you because I know it, I've seen it, and I understand it.

I know that as you come to accept the doctrines that are in the Scriptures and you understand the principles by which the Lord guides us, then you'll see the patterns more clearly.

You'll wake up to the reality of the day that you live in, and also of the excitement of the day that we live in. It's both the Great and Dreadful day that will come upon us. I hope that everyone that's listening will choose to make it a great day, instead of a dreadful one. Having said that, I think it's time to wrap it up.

Eric, do you have anything else to add?

Eric: I have one final thought from Joel 2:32, for anybody who is a little afraid of things that may be coming. It says: "And it shall come to pass, that whosoever shall call on the name of the Lord shall be delivered: for in mount Zion and in Jerusalem shall be deliverance, as the Lord hath said, and in the remnant whom the Lord shall call."

I appreciate that promise from Joel. If we just call on the Lord, we can be safe from the things that lie ahead.

Julie: Thank you for that comment, Eric. I appreciate it. I always like it when you bring Scripture into support the conversations we've had. Thanks to both of you for your time today, and I look forward to another podcast. That's all, folks.

Podcast 9

Learning of Christ

Julie: Welcome to the Julie Rowe Show. I want to introduce our guest David on the line, and we also have Eric helping us facilitate this phone call today, and this recording. I'd like to go ahead and get started.

For those that haven't listened to a podcast before, I just want to remind you that I usually have invited a guest to be on the line. I do not know the questions that will be asked. I prefer it this way. I do know a general topic that we briefly discussed right before this recording. David is the one who came up with the topic of choice today. So welcome, David.

David: Thank you, Julie. Good to be with you.

Julie: Eric, welcome to you too. Thanks for all the work you're doing. Okay, let's go ahead and get started.

David: Well, the topic we're going to talk about today is the historical and ongoing mission of Jesus Christ. What I hope to achieve with you today is to help all of our listeners out there—some who may know of Jesus Christ, others who may not—truly come to know Him a little better, through the voice of your witness and the witnesses we can put together today. Based on the time frame that we're in, I think one of the most crucial issues everyone faces in the days coming ahead is to have that fuller understanding, fuller relationship, and fuller knowledge of who Jesus Christ is, and what His real mission encompasses. Would you agree?

Julie: I absolutely agree, and I'm really glad you selected this topic today. Two minutes before we started recording, I talked to David and I asked him what the topic of choice was today that he had selected, and he's picked one of my favorite topics, if not my favorite topic, which is our Older Brother Jesus Christ.

That is the reason I am doing these podcasts, because I want to invite people to come to Christ. I want to help bring Light and knowledge and understanding to those who do not have clarity as to what His role is, or will be. I also want to remind those of us that are here of the importance of the role that Christ plays in our lives whether we know it or not. So thank you, David.

David: Well, I'm going to actually start with some scriptural references. I'm going to paint three scenarios for you, and then we'll get into a discussion These are three historic scriptures that record Christ, all of them after His death and resurrection.

Julie: I love this, because that means it's not just Julie Rowe talking, or David, or Eric. This is backed up by Scripture that has been recorded for hundreds of years. They're not my words. They're the words of people who have lived in the past that have been preserved for us, so this is great. I love documentation. Thanks. Okay, go for it.

David: All right, now this is an interesting scripture. It's one of the most famous in the entire Christian world. We start with Matthew 28, starting with verse 18: "And Jesus came and spake unto them, saying, All power is given unto me in heaven and in earth. 19 Go ye therefore, and teach all nations, baptizing them in the name of the Father, and of the Son, and of the Holy Ghost."

And in verse 20 He reminds them "and, lo, I am with you alway, even unto the end of the world. Amen."

A very powerful scripture in the Christian world, where they focus on the mission of baptizing and preaching the word of God. However, in verse 18 I hear very little commentary, and we will focus a lot of our discussion today on this one phrase that I think is one of the most powerful in all of the scriptures. That's when the resurrected Savior says to His disciples "All power is given unto me in heaven and in earth." That is quite the statement, and something we should talk a little bit more about.

Julie: That's quite a bold statement, isn't it? In fact, that is so bold to think that somebody would take it upon Himself to tell unequivocally that is who He is. He absolutely knew what His identity was. He knew the role He was playing, and he knew His mission.

I can relate to that, because as I am emboldened through Jesus Christ, and as I come to understand more of my mission, I recognize that my mission is to help support His. I want to witness and testify that I know that Jesus is the Christ, and that He is absolutely who He said He was, and who He still says He is today.

David: I testify of the same, Julie. I will add that anyone who has had the privilege of an NDE, and has had the privilege of meeting the Savior, or having interaction with the Savior, will recognize instantly that feeling from His countenance of supreme love *and* supreme power. It is literally a part of Him.

Julie Rowe: It is unequivocal. There is no separating that from Christ. My interaction with Him when I had my NDEs and since, has been such a profound experience that there is no duplication for that. There is no counterfeit for that. There really are no words for the Majesty and Power that He is, and for the humility I felt in His presence because of His greatness.

I felt most profoundly the Love that emanates from Him and

His entire being, and everything that He is, and the Love that he offers each and every one of us. I don't have words for it. It should be interesting to see how this discussion goes, because if there's one thing that gets me crying it's the topic of Christ. So I'm gonna try to hold it together.

David: Okay, hopefully I can help you with that.

Julie: Crying in a good way, right? Because I love Him, and I'm grateful for Him. Crying's not a bad thing, you guys. (Laughs)

David: Well, let's just put it this way, if the tears do come, that emanation of pure love from the Savior will literally melt your heart. It will change your heart, and anyone sensitive to that might just have a few tears, or a few other emotional reactions.

Julie: Right. How do we explain that, right? I mean, just the thought of His name, if I allow myself to feel my real emotions, my heart is softened and I, almost on an automatic response, want to love other people the way He loves them. That's the power that emanates from Him throughout all Eternity. It's a beautiful lesson.

David: If I could give a comparison, think of some moment in your life when you felt the prompting of the Holy Ghost, and you felt that warmth fill your mind and your heart. You had an "a-ha moment", and some profound understanding of the Lord, the Plan of Salvation, or something important in your life came to you through that warmth. Then multiply it by about 100 or 1,000 and you might begin to get an idea.

Julie: For me, it's untouchable right now. I have so far to go to become more like Him, but you do get a little glimpse. We get glimpses all the time, right? If there are those listening to this podcast who have never been taught about Christ or have not had a belief in Christ, or don't understand His origin or His divine mission, I want you to think what it feels like to have a family member or a friend do an act of service for you. To try to extrapolate that and put meaning to it when there are no words, when your heart has been touched in a manner that you can't even express it because you are so overwhelmed with joy and gratitude because someone has done a kind act for you. That's a tiny fragment of a feeling that you might get if you were to stand in the presence of the Lord.

David: That is a beautiful way to put it, Julie. I would back you up on that by saying that to feel that, to know that, and to understand Him is to want to be more like Him.

Now if there was ever a figure in your life, in the Universe to look up to, that understanding of Christ instantly transforms an individual into wanting to strive to become more like Him. We know that's a process that's going to go on *way* beyond mortality.

Julie: What's come to my mind, of course, are flashbacks to when I had my 2004 NDE. I don't talk about it in my book, other than to mention that I was in the presence of Father and of the Savior.

I don't talk about that in my book for several reasons. One being that I was instructed by the Spirit that people just weren't ready to hear what happened to me on several levels.

The other reason being it was such a personal, sacred experience that wasn't something I felt like I wanted to open up to the public, especially to their ridicule. But I do have specific memories. I have memories of us in the Heavens, if you will, in the Spirit World before we came to Earth. I have memories of that Heavenly Home, and I have memories of my NDE.

I had experiences growing up where the Spirit would testify to me and witness to me that I wasn't alone, that I had a loving Father in Heaven, that I had an Older Brother Jesus Christ, and that no matter what happened to me in my life, they would be there for me even when it felt like I was alone.

I have had periods of darkness. I've had several periods of

loneliness, feeling like I was abandoned and other emotions that have come up. I think we all do to varying degrees just by living on the Earth and not being in our Heavenly Home, which is our place of origin.

But when I had my 2004 NDE, and I was reminded in a very real way of that love, and the Savior reminded me of the mission that I have. He said that He trusted me. That meant more than I can even expound upon, because I remember those words.

I remember the scene that went with it. I remember the warmth of Him hugging me, and I remember some other very personal things.

Here I go, I'm going to start crying as I remember my relationship with the Savior, because I love Him with all of my heart. I know that He loves me, and I know that He loves each and every one of us. He wants us to come Home. He wants us to be happy. He wants us to feel joy, and He wants us to know and believe in The Atonement, which is His sacrifice as part of His mission to be able to fulfill Father's plan.

I know that with my whole heart. I know with every fiber of my being that God Atoned for our sins. He sacrificed so that we might be Healed and become whole one day.

That is what gives me joy and peace. That's what calms my heart in times of anguish, times of sorrow, and in times when I feel fearful or any other kind of negative emotion because of living on this Earth and being subjected to the adversary.

I just am overwhelmed with gratitude for Him and for His mission. I want to do all in my power to witness and testify of Him so that I can help other people see how great He is.

David: That's again beautifully put. Let's move to one of the other scriptures I have here, which comes out of the Doctrine and Covenants section 76, as you sit here and give your witness. I should mention that as you talked about things you didn't include in your book, we have the Prophet Joseph Smith's testimony standing before the world, and that testimony is still very narrowly received and often ridiculed by the world as it is now. I would venture to put to you it would be pretty important for that testimony to soften the hearts and be received before any other testimony can get in there.

Julie: I'm here to witness that Joseph Smith also did see Father and the Savior. That was one of many scenes that I was shown and reminded of. Upon meeting Joseph, my heart was softened. While not a perfect man, he was and is absolutely stellar in living the Gospel and in trying to help others come to Christ. He had a stewardship then and he has a stewardship now.

I agree with you. There are a lot of people on this planet who ridicule Joseph Smith. They don't understand his mission, but there will be other records that will come forth in the Latter Days prior to the Lord's second coming when the 144,000 are called upon and the tribes return. I testify that I have seen those records that will come forth. I haven't had them opened up unto me, but they have shown me that they are coming forth. I know that they will. I believe that they will.

I know that those records testify—some of which will be disclosed or opened up to us in our minds as the veil becomes thinner—that Joseph Smith is and was a true and living prophet of God.

David: Perfect. Doctrine and Covenants, section 76, verses 22 through 24: Joseph Smith and Sidney Rigdon in their opening of the Vision of the Three Degrees of Glory he said: "And now, after the many testimonies which have been given or Him, this is the testimony, last of all, which we give of Him:" speaking of Christ, "That He lives! For we saw Him, even on the right hand of God; and we heard the voice bearing record that He is the Only Begotten of the Father—That by Him, and through Him, and of Him, the worlds are and were created, and the inhabitants thereof are begotten sons and daughters unto God." What a beautiful testimony.

Julie: I want to add my witness to that, and also what Joseph Smith talked about with the Three Degrees of Glory. Within each of those Degrees of Glory there are degrees upon degrees, or line upon line of progression. He gave us the elementary school level of understanding of the Eternities, because that's what people were ready for, but I need to testify that there is so much more that goes into that which are veiled from our eyes.

We had education on it before we came to Earth, and we will then yet again be taught and reminded of that which we learned about the Eternities before we came, but I do know because I have been to other places. Now people are going to mock me for saying that. Some will wanna cast stones, but I stand by that witness. I know there are other worlds that have been and will be created, that are being created, and that we have an eternal realm that we can return to if we are faithful to the Lord.

Many of us lived in similar places together, some of us in locations prior to coming to this Earth where we knew each other. How else can people explain where they come across or meet someone and they look so familiar, or their voice resonates, or they have an instant connection, or it's like they feel like they've known them forever? It's because they *have* known that person for a very long time, and the Lord is bringing those people together and orchestrating His plan here on the earth. It is a magnificent plan. It's just amazing to me.

David: Julie, your testimony again is wonderful and is supported completely by the scriptures. Isn't it interesting that there is only one place in the scriptures where the cosmology you just described is laid out. It is not in the Old Testament or the New Testament, or even The Book of Mormon. It's the Book of Moses, in The Pearl of Great Price, where in Moses 1:37 Moses is in vision with the Lord: "And the Lord God spake unto Moses, saying: The heavens, they are many, and they cannot be numbered unto man; but they are numbered unto me, for they are mine. And as one earth shall pass away, and the heavens thereof even so shall another come; and there is no end to my works, neither to my words."

Julie: I appreciate that documentation, and here's one of the reasons why. I've had people email me and come up to me when I was speaking. They'd say they don't think I'm a true messenger because God doesn't work this way. I am here to tell people boldly, absolutely He works this way.

Who are we to limit God? He doesn't limit us, and so we shouldn't be limiting Him on how He chooses to facilitate His plan There are so many witnesses across the planet. If we could communicate with people across the planet, or if we lived in a culture and in an environment where we felt safe to open up and share spiritual things of a nature like I'm sharing, how different a people would we be if we knew that it was safe for us to tell people what was really going on in our hearts and in our minds? It would transform the Universe.

David: It would transform everything. I'll tell you what, as this will eventually be a YouTube podcast, I will put another name out there, if you don't mind, a witness that agrees completely with your witness, that can be found on YouTube: a Messianic Jew named Maurice Sklar. There's a witness from a completely different background and religious upbringing. If you type him in on YouTube, or Google, he will give a witness that will agree almost a hundred percent with your witness, Julie. The Lord is no respecter of persons.

Julie: I've never heard of him until just now, but I believe it because the Lord is no respecter of persons. If He's going to show me, He could show anyone this.

David: Again, no respecter of persons. What that really means is the Lord loves everybody equally, and gives them the equal chance to come unto Him. But we were talking about the three degrees of glory briefly. Let's circle that back around to our main subject of Jesus Christ. What is the primary criteria for our life after this life? It is, in fact, our cognitive choice, both temporal and spiritual, to receive the Gospel of Jesus Christ and to form our lives according to its precepts.

Julie: So how do we do that? Let me ask the audience that, as you take charge upon your heart. How do you do that? How do you come unto Christ? How do you make Christ the center in your life? How do you give up Babylon or anything that is holding you back from becoming who you were divinely created to become?

David: In coming to know Christ is choosing to seek Him and reach out. The first step in coming to any knowledge is to exercise that particle of faith that maybe this knowledge you are seeking might indeed have some validity or some proof to it and reach out and begin to search for that truth.

That's the beauty of mortality. We have the choice every minute of every day to govern our thoughts, our desires and our actions. And the first step is to simply reach out. And you know as well as anyone who knows the Savior that if you extend your hand and you sincerely reach towards Him, don't be surprised if He takes your hand.

Julie: Right. I appreciate that. So taking your hand can come in a lot of different scenarios. In my experience, before I had my NDE in 2004, I was already converted to Christ. I had been since being a young child, and I had line upon line teaching as I grew up. You can learn about that on my website as well as in some of these other podcasts.

But prior to my NDE, just before I went into the hospital, I was dealing with some very strong emotion and some things in my personal life that I was trying to clear up. I had some relationships in my life that were causing me heartache, and I wanted to be able to feel like I was clean before the Lord. There was nothing really weighing on my heart that I felt like was huge, that I needed to repent of, but there were lots of little things that kind of nagged at me. I felt like there was more I could do and more I could learn about the Savior to be able to apply the Atonement.

A few days before I went into the hospital, I spent several hours in prayer, meditation, and scripture reading. I was crying before the Lord, and I said to Him in all sincerity: "Lord, I want nothing more than to return to You, and what I want the most is to be able to help others do the same. I don't wanna be a stumbling block. I wanna help, I wanna serve, I wanna do whatever You want me to do, whatever that is. I don't fully understand what it is, but I wanna do that."

Then I said to Him: "Whatever I have to go through, whatever I need to do to become who I need to become, and to develop the gift of charity, because without charity we're nothing."

I totally believed that scripture that without charity I was nothing, and I said to Him in all sincerity of heart: "Whatever I need to go through, even if it's an Alma the Younger or Lamoni experience, or like Joseph of Egypt or something to that affect, anything I need to go through I will go through if You will bless me with the gift of charity one day."

He took me up on it. Within a matter of a few days I was deathly ill. I was in the hospital, then I was on the other side of the veil. I was being taught about deeper doctrine than I had currently understood in mortality.

I was understanding things about my divine origin and the creation, and some of what the Lord had planned for me. He took charge, and He said to me: "You said this, do you really mean it? I believe that you do, and if you will stay the course, one day you will be blessed with charity."

That is a gift that I am grateful for, and I'm looking to develop that. It can only come through Christ.

David: Correct. Let me give you an interesting quote from one of my favorites, Dr. Hugh Nibley, and this is for our audience to ponder about how do we get to know Christ? He says: "The difference between a righteous man and a wicked man is the felt need for repentance. A person is either repenting, forsaking and improving, or they see no need for it. It is simply a matter of which direction you are facing." Any comments on that?

Julie: I find a need for it every day, every minute. When I have a thought that maybe isn't the most kind, or if I say something to my husband or my children that isn't very sensitive. Or if there are actions that are in my past that I haven't cleared up.

It happens every minute of every day, if we're repenting like we're supposed to be repenting. Ideally, it's a conscious thought, and often subconscious as we go throughout our day. It's a lot easier to do it that way than to wait and wait, and then try to unload all of it, although it's not too late for people to repent.

The atonement is infinite and eternal. Infinite meaning never ending. Eternal meaning never ending, and I believe that. I know it to be true. There are things that were hurtful that people have done to me, or that I've done to others that happened over the years, and I can tell you that the Lord absolutely can heal your heart.

It works every time. It is a foolproof method, that it was designed by the Laws of Heaven, and the justice and mercy scale is absolutely balanced when we repent.

David: Well, you've just given another perfect segue to the next comment. Everything that makes salvation and exaltation possible in the Plan of Salvation centers on the Atoning Sacrifice the Savior wrought at the end of His mortal ministry. Can you talk a little bit about the universal and far reaching implications of that Atonement and what it means to us today and in the days ahead?

Julie: Yes. The Atonement is Everlasting and Ever-Reaching throughout the Universe, and there are more planets involved here than just Earth because Christ is the Savior of several earths and several planets. It's an Infinite Atonement no matter what side of the veil you're on, whether you are an unclean or disembodied spirit, or whether you are spiritually here on the earth trying to work out your salvation unto the Lord. This is an Infinite and Eternal Atonement.

God fulfills all of His promises to His children. He will not leave you. He will not abandon you. There is nothing you have done that is too great that cannot be encompassed and healed for through the Atonement of Jesus Christ. No atrocity that you have gone through and no atrocity that you've caused that will not be taken care of, and balanced, and then therefore removed as you seek to repent and come closer to the Light.

What is required is a broken heart and contrite spirit. Broken meaning that we are humbled, that we get on our knees and we beg God, or ask Him to please help us, first of all, know what it is we need to repent of. Then second, to give us the courage and the strength to do so.

Then to learn to forgive ourselves, because once that slate has been wiped clean, the adversary tries to beat us up and tell us that we're never gonna make it, that we've done something too awful, that were not good enough, that we're never going to be good enough.

But that Gift has already been given. The Atonement has already happened. It was designed for us premortally before the world was even created. God planned for that Atonement. It's part of the Eternal Law that encompasses our missions here on Earth.

So the biggest lie Satan tells people is that the Atonement isn't real, that it doesn't exist. Then when people do believe in the Atonement, he tells them they're not worthy or they're not able or capable, that they're never gonna be good enough.

Those are lies he said that to us premortally and that he says still on Earth today, that no matter what we do we're, you know, we're not gonna be able to be Atoned. That is a lie. The other lie is that was told premortally and it's still being told, is that you don't need to have the Atonement, when in fact *you do*.

The Atonement and acknowledging Christ is key to Salvation, and it's key to happiness in the Eternities. It enters you in at the gate once you've been baptized. Once people wake up to that reality, once they accept Christ, and once they realize that it is an equally yoked relationship going hand in hand into the Eternities to return to Father, the better off they are. Because then they put their pride aside, and they realize how much they need Christ.

They then glorify Christ, and He helps them advance in their power, knowledge and understanding of how to become more like the Lord in gaining more light and knowledge and advancing in the Light. By advancing in their progression, they are able to move on into higher worlds and higher vibrations instead of being stuck in the muck of a low vibration on a Telestial level. That was an earful, but that's what came out. (Laughs)

David: Very well put. Let's bring this a little bit around, full circle. In modern teachings the actual identity, power and role of Christ has been watered down in a lot of ways in modern religious, philosophical and pop culture thought. He's taught as a man, a myth, a good deed doer, a moralist and many other viewpoints. His divine origin, power and ongoing mission has almost been scrubbed from modern theology.

When I counsel my children or others as I'm trying to bring them closer to the Lord, I remind them of this simple psychological paradigm: Let us assume that humans do have a soul, and that soul will continue beyond the end of mortal life. If that assumption is true, what *is* truly the most important? Is it the life we currently live? Or is it the Eternities awaiting with open arms, for us all?

I would suggest it is the latter that is the most important, though we must pay attention to what we are doing here and now. And if the latter, that Eternal Life of the soul, is in fact a part of our existence and is part of who we were designed by the Father to be, maybe it's a good idea that we take the Lord at face value, and take the words and the teachings and the witnesses that have been given us of Him at face value, and start from there.

Julie: I agree. A few things came to mind when you were

mentioning that. I would encourage those who are listening, if you are struggling in your understanding or knowledge of Christ, or you are struggling in your belief, or even anything to do with wanting to acknowledge His existence, I say take it to the Source. Test it upon this method, and that is to get on your knees.

If you've never prayed before, it's not too late to pray now. Get on your knees, specifically direct a prayer to Father in Heaven, and ask Him in all sincerity if Jesus is the Christ. When you do that, whether it's immediate or not, I promise you there will come an answer, and it comes in different ways.

One of the most profound ways that it comes is with a calm feeling in the heart, a warmth that comes through you. That is one of the most common ways—to feel peace. That will be an answer to you that I speak truth, that Christ is the Savior, and that you need to go ahead and study more upon His words and find out more about His mission.

If it doesn't come immediately, don't give up, because sometimes we're just really blocked by the dark energy that's trying to keep us from understanding the role we play in the Eternities. One of the biggest lies Satan tells is that we don't need Christ, because we are getting closer to the Second Coming and this battle is raging. It's been raging for a long time on the spiritual front. Why is it that this role of Christ has been watered down, even in theology?

I would basically like to put that question out there, because when we're honest in our attempt to find the answers, we don't give up until we get them. When we ask the question and we go to the effort and do the work to find the answer, *God always answers*. Sometimes I have things that have bothered me, or I've had questions and concerns for years, and they're not answered for a long time.

Other times they're answered right away. I have answers to prayers that happened this week that I prayed about forty years ago when I was a little four-year-old little girl. Questions and concerns I had that are now being answered. I think if that's how it's gonna work, then the Lord always answers and maybe I just wasn't ready for that answer until I was forty-four. Heavenly Father, in His wisdom, knows when we need those answers. That is my witness and testimony. David, do you have anything else to say about that, or anything you want to add? I think it's about time for us to wrap up this call.

David: I'll give you a little wrap up here. Joseph Smith once said: "All the things that Joseph has seen, the least of the Saints may see as soon as they are prepared."

That goes hand in hand with what the Savior said in John 14:12. He said: "Verily, verily I say unto you he that believeth on me, the works that I do shall he do also. And greater works than these shall he do, because I go unto my Father."

Julie: Right.

David: The Lord loves us. The Lord wants us to reach out to Him. As He does, as both the Savior Himself and as modern day prophets have said, He will empower you to become more like Him and act in the ways that He does. So where do you start? You start with a kernel of faith. And where can you eventually end up? Well, we have some witnesses to that.

Julie: I appreciate that. I appreciate your witness and your testimony. I want to add when it comes to my story and my witness, those that are concerned, those who have questions, those that wonder if I speak truth on any level, take that to the Lord. Ask Him in all sincerity of heart, and as you do that, in time, when the Spirit is knowing that you are ready to handle the Truth that's being disclosed, that witness will come to you.

That is what I encourage for the pattern the Lord has given us. No matter what we are seeking, as we seek truth, all truth is circumscribed into one Eternal Whole and can be made known to us as we are ready for it. The Lord does not give us any more than we can handle, when we can handle it. That means everything from a trial, to a learning experience, to gaining full knowledge and understanding on a doctrine or principle.

As I share these things and witness to you, my intention is that you will turn to Christ, that you will ask Him, that you will ask questions of Him and you will be ready for the answers when He gives them. I leave this witness and testimony with you. Let's end this show and start again tomorrow.

Eric: David, very well done. Those questions were very well orchestrated.

David: Thank you. That wasn't on the sheet that I sent you, but as I was laying in bed the other night I'm like: "We gotta start with Christ and go from there."

Julie: It was very good. Very needed. It was excellent.

David: Being a convert myself, and having so many family members that have, at best, a rudimentary understanding of the Savior and worst, completely confused by the philosophies of men mingled with scripture, it is a subject near and dear to my heart.

You know, you talk about missionary work in some of the other podcasts. What is missionary work? Getting people to begin that relationship and truly come to *know* the Savior, not just know of Him.

Julie: Right. Well, hopefully this podcast will help soften some hearts and give them a little insight.

David: Great job, Julie. Your heart is as big as the ocean.

Julie: Thank you David, thank you Eric. Well, I'd better wrap it up. Thanks for your time today.

PODCAST 10

⚜

THE GATHERING: SAFETY IN THE "CALLOUT"

Julie: Hi, welcome to the Julie Rowe Show. Today I've got my friend Eric on the line and we're gonna talk about a very important topic. Eric, how are you today?

Eric: Doing great. I'm looking forward to this subject today, Julie. Thanks for giving me the chance again to ask you about some of my questions and my thoughts.

I wanna just start by telling my own background with relation to your books and your message. Before I read your books, in about 2014, I had read another book that talked about the days ahead and some of the calamities and trials that we would face. One of those was the plagues.

I remember getting really apprehensive about the plagues. I was a little nervous and scared. That energy just kind of hung there until I read your books. My wife was reading to me, and she described something that was very peculiar to me. It was this idea of a gathering, and instantly my worries were brushed away. It was like: "Yes! I always knew the Lord had a plan to protect and save His children during those hard times."

So that's the premise for this conversation. This subject is sometimes referred to as the Call Out, or The Gathering. I just wanted to give you a chance to talk about this.

Julie: Well, I appreciate this topic. It's one that is at the forefront of my thoughts, and it's a layered topic. The verbiage that's been given to me is to call it The Gathering, so I wanted to clarify that for sure.

A lot of people refer to it as the Call Out because some of what the other people have been shown in dream and vision. They have seen that the Prophet of the LDS Church will call members of the Church to gather to places of safety. So that's what we're referring to when we talk about the Call Out.

So if you hear me in this podcast or other podcasts refer to The Gathering, that's what we're talking about. They're one in the same, but the Call Out is inclusive of the Gathering. The Gathering includes the Call Out as well as a whole lot more than that.

So first and foremost, I have been shown many times both in my NDE's and in dream and vision that there will be a Gathering of Saints of the LDS Church in the Last Days. There will also be a Gathering of people from all walks of life in different forms and fashions in communities and congregations throughout the world.

When we will refer to this on the podcast as the Call Out, we are specifically referring to members of the LDS Faith who are invited by the Presidency of the Church of Jesus Christ of Latter-day Saints to gather in camps and other safe locations in preparation for the Days of Tribulation.

Eric: I'm the author of a little blog. It's got a very humble following, but I've posted on a number of topics, particularly religious topics. It's called: **DoctrinalEssays.Blogspot.com**.

Julie: It's a great blog. I encourage anyone that's listening to go to Eric's blog. It's actually very profound. He has some really good doctrinal insights.

Eric: (Laughs) Thanks Julie. Well, most of my posts at best will get a meager number of views, so I was surprised to find that one post on there called "The Doctrinal Significance of the Call Out" has several thousand views. It is totally off the charts for me.

I'm bringing this up not to say that I've done something wonderful. I'm really trying to point out is that in my humble writings, people have taken an interest in that topic. It's not that I'm a great writer, it's just a fascinating topic. Why do you think people are so interested in this idea of gathering?

Julie: Well, first of all I have to say you are a great writer. For those that are wondering how I know that, I've read all of the posts on Eric's blog, and Eric is writing my biography. So I know firsthand that Eric's a great writer, he's just very humble and modest in that.

But in answer to your question, I think there are a lot of reasons why people are interested. There have been a few different books that have come out about The Gathering. In dreams, visions and NDE's, people have been shown that this Gathering will take place. There have been a lot of people that have contacted me about it.

Some people maybe have only one dream or vision, but sometimes people have had several. There are a lot of people that have questions about what this means, and they're curious why the Lord would be showing them something like this.

When they read about my story and hear the podcasts or radio shows, their curiosity is piqued because they're trying to place meaning on what this could mean for them, and their friends and family. There's a lot of concern, fear, and worry related to this.

I just talked to somebody who was concerned that they were gonna be left behind. They have a lot of fear energy, worrying that something's gonna happen in the world and the Prophet will issue an Invitation to Gather, and they won't hear about it for some reason.

I'm here to tell you that no matter what happens to us, we need to trust that it's the Lord's plan. The Lord has a lot of different ways that He gets his messages out, including the Invitation to Gather. It won't be a one-time shot.

I see this Gathering happening over the course of a three to four month period. Some people are invited and they go within 24 to 48 hours. Others go within 72 hours, while some people go within a few weeks.

Then there are people like myself who will stay where they are. I'll have people coming through my property on their way to go to a Gathering Place. My property is just one of many safe houses for people to come through and stop on their way. I don't end up going west for about four months after the initial Call comes from the Brethren.

Eric: You don't see this as just like a one-time event. So it isn't like: "Here you go, everybody. Come on," and then it's done.

Julie: No, I see it happening in waves, although I don't know the parameters that are gonna be given. I have an understanding of some of the requirements, guidelines, and boundaries that are gonna be set. I don't have permission to go into specifics as to what some of those are.

However, we can discuss some of that today to give clarity, and to dispel myths and get rid of fear energy. There are a lot of lies that the adversary tells people. His main motive with this is to keep as many people as possible from Gathering, because the more people that gather, the more possibility that righteousness will be on the Earth to combat the forces of evil. He doesn't want members of the LDS Church, or any person at all, to become a stronger, more valiant person.

Much of the reason that these Gathering experiences will happen is to unify communities, to help people, families, and friends unify for the cause of Zion. This will help people become perfected in Christ.

There are a lot of reasons why we will gather and there are a lot of reasons why the adversary doesn't want the information to get out to people in general of what's gonna happen. That way he can cause more fear and generate negative energy that is not healthy.

Instead of making it a cause for reflection and faith, he can have people put it aside, because they're so afraid they don't want to look at it at all.

Eric: Interesting. You're making me think of something Joseph Smith said: "In addition to all temporal blessings, there is no other way for the Saints to be saved in these last days than by Gathering." It makes me wonder if Joseph had a sense of how this would all culminate here in these Latter Days.

Julie: He did. He was a Prophet, Seer, and Revelator, and he's taking part on the other side of the veil very actively regarding the Gathering. He is also involved on the other side of the veil with missionary work, leading armies and spiritual warfare. He absolutely is still a leader on the other side of the veil, and he has insight and foresight as to what is coming for us.

We believe as members of the Church that Joseph Smith was a true Prophet, and we have to take his words at face value. The same goes with Brigham Young and other Church leaders. If people were to read the *Journal of Discourses*, they would find that there are quite a few references to the topic of the Gathering.

It says the same things in the Scriptures. If you look at the patterns that the Lord has in both the Bible and the Book of Mormon, He does call His people out and He does call them to repentance. He does do it for several reasons, like providing safety in times of affliction, or to escape the destruction of cities and other areas.

Eric: It appears that there are even references to this very Gathering in other parts of Scripture, like Isaiah 26:20-21.

It reads: "20 Come, my people, enter thou into thy chambers and shut thy doors about thee: Hide thyself as it were for a little moment, until the indignation be overpast. 21 For, behold, the Lord cometh out of his place to punish the inhabitants of the Earth for their iniquity: The Earth also shall disclose her blood, and she'll no more cover her slain."

Isaiah is saying to go to your chambers and escape the calamities during this time of persecution and tribulation. There are other prophets who've made references in ancient Scripture, so it seems like a really significant thing.

Julie: Right. And even the word "chambers" is layered in meaning. It is as if Isaiah was speaking code language, which is gonna become essential in the Last Days for many people to survive. There will be everything from foreign troops coming in, to marauders and others that would seek harm.

When I think of secret chambers I think not only of hiding up in places of safety in a physical sense, but I think of us going to the secret chambers of our heart. It means looking at the heart of the matter, and really pondering upon the word of God and upon the Scriptures. They are written by His servants to give the underlying reasons why people would gather, and it is sound doctrine that has been passed down throughout all generations of time.

Eric: That's really good. Okay, I have a question. Over the years I've had friends in the Church that I've talked about this. In the early days of the Church, when they lived in Nauvoo and back east, they obviously went through this trekking time period. They moved West, and they brought their handcarts and settled the Salt Lake Valley.

Almost in jest, some of my friends will say: "Oh yeah, I'm sure one day we're all gonna walk back to Missouri with our handcarts." They kind of laugh about it like it's a big joke, and I think it's because they're thinking, "Our technology is so amazing these days we're just gonna drive back." But I don't know about that. Do you have any thoughts on that?

Julie: I do have thoughts on that. I have been shown that very thing, that the Saints will walk back. Some individuals will be translated, and they will help others walk back. We'll have angelic, and resurrected, and translated beings on the Earth when that time comes. They will help the Saints who are still in mortality who are returning from the mountain areas and going to Jackson County, Missouri.

This is a doctrine that is unique to the LDS faith. It's bold for the LDS faith to say it, and they've been highly persecuted over the years for claiming that they would have stewardship of certain ordinances and certain doctrines. But I testify and witness to you that it is a true principle, that the Saints will return to Jackson County, Missouri after a cleansing occurs there.

That is a separate topic that we'll discuss later when we go back through different parts of the United States. But it's important for people to realize that when the Madrid fault line slips and the inland ocean is created, the Missouri and Mississippi rivers will flow backward. They will flood not only Jackson County, but the surrounding areas in the Kansas City area and going up north through Iowa and into the Great Lakes area.

That monstrous earthquake starts in the Gulf of Mexico and goes all the way up the Madrid fault. It has multiple impact points. When the Madrid goes it's at least a 9.5, maybe a 10.0 on the Richter scale. It's so huge that it creates the inland ocean from the waters of the Missouri and Mississippi rivers. That's not unprecedented. There have been times in history when this has occurred before.

Then other earthquakes splinter off, causing major damage and flooding additional areas. I live an hour and fifteen minutes from the Kansas City Missouri LDS Temple. I have seen in the future that my neighborhood will be flooded. I live in the country, but there are houses that are about a quarter of a mile from my house. I live on a hill, and the water will not reach my house. We purposely bought this house on a hill. We won't get wet, because we're elevated, but the land down below our home where my quarter-mile driveway is will be flooded. I have been shown that many times. The earthquakes will open up aquifers and they will cleanse the area.

So back to the Gathering. We are already gathering together as

Stakes and Wards in a physical sense in different parts of the world. We will be gathered to the Mountain West in the United States, and in other countries, the Saints will go to their mountain areas as well.

Even in Hawaii the Saints will flee to the mountainous region and to the temple grounds. So this Gathering will happen all over the world, and it happens in real time. We're gonna increasingly see this.

There will be an invitation from the Prophet for those living in the mainland of the United States to come to the Mountain West. They will go to girls camps and other places of safety to gain refuge from The Storm. This will affect not only the Saints, but also the millions of people that are going to come into those valleys seeking refuge once the disasters happen and civil unrest begins.

The gathering will help the Saints survive the tribulations, ranging from the plagues to war, to civil unrest, to natural disasters.

The Elders of Israel will eventually come down from the mountains to combat the enemy force. They will have a standoff in Grand Junction, Colorado, and later in the Denver area.

Once our enemy forces have been defeated by the Elders of Israel, then we will be able to pave a way to Zion. I've seen the path the Elders will clear for the Saints to start returning back to Jackson County.

That will happen toward the end of the tribulations, starting as early as three to four years into the tribulations, but it will be toward the tail end of the seven years before larger groups of the Saints return to Jackson County.

When that Gathering occurs, the 144,000 begins their missions and the return of the Ten Lost Tribes starts. They will also help with this Gathering. Then we will start transitioning into things like the Church of The Firstborn, preparatory to Christ's Coming.

Eric: That's awesome. You said that those who are blessed enough to go back and settle the New Jerusalem will walk there. Do you see any motorized transportation to help?

Julie: I do see some vehicles, but most people do not have motorized transportation. I do see airplanes and helicopters, and I actually see some really cool aircraft. So there are other methods of transportation, but the majority of what I see is people going on foot.

Eric: Okay, you've mentioned New Jerusalem. How long does it take to build this new city?

Julie: Several years. When the war is finished, I'm living in Idaho and I go back and forth to the Midwest for about three years. I'm being told by the Spirit that I will be in Idaho for at least three years before I go to New Jerusalem. So that's at the tail end of the Tribulations.

Once the end of the Tribulations occur, I don't know how long it is from the time I'm in my house in New Jerusalem until Christ comes, because none of us know when the Savior comes. But I see us actively building New Jerusalem for many years until Christ's Second Coming when He actually takes over the Kingdom and becomes the Rightful Heir.

I don't know how long that is. It could be three or ten years, it could be twenty years. I don't have any idea how long we're living in New Jerusalem until the Kingdom is actually established with Christ taking His rightful place here on the earth.

There's got to be enough time that we can build the Temple of New Jerusalem. Then there's 12 temples that surround the New Jerusalem Temple and then another 12 temples that go out from there that make up the Center Stake of Zion.

So that takes some time, but you'll have angelic, resurrected, and translated beings as well as mortals working on it. We'll also construct homes and businesses. I say businesses because we will still operate as a society. We won't have the Babylonian system, but we will still be in business with trade, and we will still be merchandising in the sense of the Heavenly Order of things. There will be universities built and other schools. People will be doing a lot of different types of healing, and lots of genealogy work. It will be a very busy, active place.

Eric: That is so much fun to think about. I'm glad we went on that little tangent for a minute.

Let me pull us back to the Call Out. I guess the Call Out functions as a safe mechanism for those who are faithful during the days of tribulation. Is that fair to say?

Julie: It is, but we don't want any grand illusions that safe means easy, or that safe means you're going to avoid the plague or something else. In general we will be protected compared to those on the outside. Those people in the cities will really be struggling.

But we will still experience starvation, frostbite, and in some cases the plague. We will still have to deal with foreign troops dropping bombs and other things, but for the most part, due to the Gathering of the Saints and their righteousness and priesthood protection, we will be blessed. We will be protected in ways that people cannot even imagine, because of the miracles that will happen.

Eric: Interesting. That's so comforting. Can you take us into a day of life during Call Out conditions?

Julie: Well, it depends if you're living in a home and you have people coming to your property seeking refuge, or if you're living in a tent in a girl's camp. I think some people need to realize that those camps are not just set up for members of the Church.

Actually, a lot of the people that come to those camps later on will be refugees who are not LDS that need a safe place to come as well. So we need to have our hearts and our minds open to that, realizing there are a lot of reasons why we have been instructed by the Church to have a year supply of food.

It's not just for our family. We need to be welcoming those

that need food, clothing and shelter. I've been shown many scenes of the girls camp situations. I don't wanna limit it to girls camps, though, because we have a lot of people that have seen in dreams and visions of their own where there are dozens of people camping in tents on their property. I will be one of those families that has that happen at my place. I've been told to prepare for up to fifty families at a time on my twenty acres.

That's a monumental task to prepare my property as a way station, as well as try to come up with the funding and supplies to be able to accomplish this at our other safe houses.

There are safe houses in our GTRF organization that will have thousands upon thousands of people come through. Some may only come in for a drink of water or a short, quick meal. Others might stay for a night, and some might be living there for up to two years.

Eric: Interesting.

Julie: When it comes to The Gathering, a lot of people want to know why the Church would do something about this. What is the importance of gathering together? There are so many lessons that will be learned, and so many miracles.

You asked a question about what I see in the camps. Well, I see that observing the Sabbath Day is absolutely critical, now *and* then, in regard to actual physical and spiritual survival. That commandment cannot be separated from the physical protection that will be given.

For instance, when manna is provided in some of those locations like it was provided in the days of Moses leading the Israelites out of Egypt, we will see those miracles in modern day as well. When cupboards need to be replenished because you're on your last bit of food in your pantry and you still have more people coming through asking for food, praying upon that food is absolutely critical. You never wanna eat anything if you haven't prayed for it, including water.

Then we'll watch miracles unfold, similar to the days of Christ when He was able to multiply food, like the story of the fish and the loaves of bread feeding the five thousand. Those are real stories that were put in the Scriptures for a reason.

We're supposed to liken them to our day, so I encourage people to study those Scripture stories. Also, have faith that the Lord has a plan.

But when it comes to keeping the Sabbath Day holy, I can't emphasize that enough. I was shown many times that manna would be provided on a Saturday with the instruction that they were to collect enough for Sunday, but not to go out on Sunday. Sadly, it often played out exactly like the story of the Israelites.

I encourage you to go look at that story again. When you are in a situation where this is presented to you, I encourage you to make sure that you are following the Sabbath Day. That includes not going out and doing any work when you're in those survival situations that doesn't absolutely have to be done.

Obeying that commandment will strengthen your body, and it'll give you additional health and protection. It may even protect you from the plague.

I have seen real protection in keeping the Sabbath Day holy, from the plagues to protection against foreign troops and other things. It is a doctrine that will save lives.

Eric: When you say that observing the Sabbath Day will provide protection, I've always thought of it in more spiritual terms. I'm starting to see that with the Tribulations and even today, these spiritual blessings really come to our aid physically as well.

Julie: Right. We have spiritual laws that are physical laws. We really can't separate the two. We need to unify our spirits with the Lord's will, and therefore unify our spirit and body together.

Everything is spirit matter. We have physical matter, but spirit matter is also a form of protection for us. Think of putting on the armor of God and shielding ourselves. I've encouraged people to go to Ephesians, and to Isaiah, and to the Doctrine and Covenants and other parts of scripture you learn about putting on the whole armor of God. It's going to be absolutely critical in the days ahead.

It's critical now, but it will be increasingly critical for people to learn how to accurately shield themselves and protect themselves from a lot of different spiritual warfare that's gonna come their way.

Eric: Interesting. When I think of the Call Out or The Gathering. I think of it being a covering or a protection. I used to do a little research in Hebrew words, and I found out the word atonement actually means covering. It's like a covering of our sins, and it feels to me The Gathering is really a way of covering us from our days ahead.

Julie: I love that analogy. I think that's great. The Atonement is the only way. It is what will protect us, in a very real physical sense. It is what helps heal our hearts now, and later.

That leads us to the topic of The Gathering in the spirit realm. Whether we're on this side of the veil or the other side of the veil, The Gathering allows us to come home and to be gathered in as the Lord's people and as His children.

The Lord requires a broken heart and a contrite spirit, and that is where the Atonement comes in. He heals our hearts and a big part of my mission is to help open and heal the hearts of the children of men. That refers to men, women, and children in opening and healing their hearts.

As we open our hearts to the Word of God, we open our hearts to the concept of The Gathering, and we open our hearts to Christ. That is the first step to being able to recognize that there is no other way other than Christ, and that He wants to gather us home.

Eric: That's awesome.

Julie: I think with that, Eric, that we can wrap it up. Do you have anything else that you want to say today?

Eric: I have a final thought. I have been thinking also about the Abrahamic Covenant. We read about that in the Scriptures, in the Bible and the Pearl of Great Price, and so forth.

Nephi also talks a lot about it, and so did the Savior. One thing I've learned about it is that Abraham was continually tested. He went through great periods of hardship, and he just seemed to always have passed his tests. I wonder if you have a way of likening that to the Days of Tribulation for those who are on the Earth.

Julie: I think that's an excellent point, because in the personal revelation that I have received about my life regarding what I've already been called upon to endure and will yet endure, I have been told I will have several Abrahamic tests. As I endure those, specific blessings have been promised to me as I endure each one.

Everyone, from my understanding, will have at least one Abrahamic test as part of this Gathering, and several of us will have many. In my case, I will have quite a few, but with those come amazing blessings. They allow us to heal and come closer to Christ if we allow it to happen that way in our lives. I know that the Lord's work is absolutely worth it.

Eric: Thanks, Julie. The things you've seen and shared with us give me hope. I hope it gives other people hope about the future, and not to worry too much about the hard times. I feel like those hard times will help cleanse and purify us, and also prepare us for the Second Coming of our Savior.

Julie: Right. We came to Earth to be able to learn how to progress in our spiritual progression. We are learning what it is to be more like the Savior and thereby learn what we need to become in order to return to our Father in Heaven and progress into the Eternities.

This is just one step, but it's a big step that we're taking as we go through this life. Just remember that before we came to Earth, we were foreordained to live during this time so that we could accomplish the Lord's purposes. The main purpose He has for you is that He wants you return home. And I say that in His name. Thank you so much Eric. It has been a great podcast, and I look forward to doing another one with you.

Bonus Section

---❖---

The Doctrinal Significance of the Callout

by Eric J. Smith

(Originally posted on **DoctrinalEssays.Blogspot.com**)

Throughout the history of good and evil on earth there have been many key moments when evil might have prevailed over righteousness had the Lord not intervened. Such times demonstrate the Lord's tender mercy to the righteous, along with his vengeance upon the wicked. But despite his miraculous ability to protect and preserve he has always used practical means of separating the righteous from the wicked before exercising judgment. Such will be the case again in a future event. "The Callout", as it has come to be known in some circles, will offer protection during the Days of Tribulation to those who hear the Lord's voice, and it will safely lead many of the elect who harden not their hearts into the Millennium (see Doctrine and Covenants 43:29).

The Callout is not widely discussed or understood. Just enough has been revealed to start conversation and lead to speculation. Those who have not studied this subject may think of it as a future event when the saints spontaneously walk or drive back to

Independence Missouri and build the New Jerusalem. While that special reverse exodus will certainly occur, a few leaders have made comments clarifying how that event will, and will not happen [1] [2]. Having studied many of those sources, I get the feeling that some of the brethren have seen and know of a call to gather and are planning its details at this time; possibly since the time of Joseph the Prophet. I can only validate this thought through the feelings that have come as I've pondered and researched this doctrine.

Modern day revelation includes other sources as well. Dallin H. Oaks has taught that there are those prophets among us who do not hold the "prophetic office" [3], but possess the prophetic gifts of dreams, and revelation (see Joel 2:28; Acts 2:18). Some from this group have shared their insights publicly, and the spirit readily confirms their truthfulness to me. Still, having believed and felt the truthfulness of these accounts, I have validated many of their details with what has been revealed through priesthood channels and scripture, and have found them to be doctrinally and scripturally sound. From my studies of the Callout, I conclude the following:
• The Callout is scriptural and is the grand culminating event of a familiar pattern found throughout scripture.
• The Callout is doctrinal.
• The Callout is temporal and spiritual - meaning, it pertains to our physical and spiritual protection and welfare.
• The Callout is tied to the Abrahamic Covenant, in that it will test God's children as Abraham was tested and proven, and it is evidence that the Father intends to honor His covenants with Abraham, Isaac, and Jacob, in preserving their seed.
• At its core, the Callout is about the redeeming and overpowering aspects of the Atonement of the Savior Jesus Christ. It will bring deliverance to modern members of the House of Israel in the same way the children of Israel were passed over by the destroying angel, escaping death and destruction.

Scriptural

There are many scriptural accounts of righteous and obedient saints being led away from wickedness to lands of promise. Noah is an obvious example, as well as the Jaredites who fled the wicked builders of Babel's tower. Abraham left his inheritance in Ur of the Chaldees among idolatrous priests to the promised land of Canaan. Joseph of Egypt provided protection to his family in Canaan from a horrible seven year famine. The Israelites, Lehi (and numerous other Book of Mormon stories), and even the saints in the early days of The Restoration moved from their places of Babylonian lifestyles and persecution in pursuit of protection. These events and others testify of the scriptural pattern the Lord uses to protect his covenant people who hear his voice.

Doctrinal

Knowing Independence, Missouri to be the central place, as described in Doctrine and Covenants, it stands to reason that there will be many who go back to Independence, Missouri at some point to begin construction of the New Jerusalem Temple, and that great city of righteousness. But to assume that saints will be at their day job one day, and then trekking to the modern day Promised Land the next day to build the holiest temple and city of all time is naive and doctrinally lacking. Before such a trying, historic, significant, and holy undertaking is made, the people doing the work must be sanctified. "My people must be tried in all things, that they may be prepared to receive the glory that I have for them, even the glory of Zion; and he that will not bear chastisement is not worthy of my kingdom" (Doctrine and Covenants 136: 31).

Spiritual and Temporal

Because of the fall of Adam, we each came to a world as slaves to the devil, and we would ever be so unless a way was prepared (see Mosiah 16:5). On a more personal level, even one single sin committed in a lifetime would be enough to prevent each soul from returning to the Father unless a way was prepared. We are completely dependent upon the Savior in order to redeem us from the fall of Adam.

Twice a year without fail, my five children remind me how helpless we are in preventing the flu, common colds, and other communicable diseases. And inevitably, when one of us gets it, we all get it. During the days of Tribulation there will be plagues (see Doctrine and Covenants 97:22-26) poured out upon mankind, not to mention all the other upheavals of nature. With regard to these temporal plagues and calamities, I feel the same helplessness and complete and total dependence upon the Savior to protect my family from them, in the same way I depend spiritually upon the Savior for redemption from sin.

Those who heed our prophet during the Callout will be blessed, and may find temporal and spiritual deliverance.

Covenants

Sanctification can come about through affliction (see Isaiah 48:10). Abraham's eternally significant covenant with the Father was only complete after a number of tests described in Genesis 12-22 (and The book of Abraham). One of the last of these tests was to dismember, wash and anoint, divide, and completely burn his son on an altar in the Olah sacrifice ritual [4]. Abraham demonstrated devotion to God in nearly offering his son, and in so doing, his covenant with the Father was sealed. This covenant now binds families together for eternity in holy temples. Members who build the New Jerusalem temple complex will have experienced similar trials of faith. For many, the tests will come during the events related to The Callout.

Abraham's faithfulness in persevering through a number of tests without faltering put the Lord in a peculiar position. The Lord had promised Abraham that he would be a father of many (righteous) nations (see Genesis 17: 4-5; Abraham 1:2; Romans 4:

17-18), that his seed would be numerous, and he and they would have temple blessings. Many aspects of this covenant are complete; some will not be entirely fulfilled until the earth is translated and many nations enter into the ordinances and covenants of exaltation (Millennium). Through Abraham's faithfulness, the Lord became bound to honor His end of the covenant to preserve Abraham's posterity through to the end times. Because of Abraham, the Lord is obligated to protect and prosper the House of Israel! Nearly every ancient prophet knew this, and rejoiced in our day when it would be fulfilled.

But there is an obstacle that needs to be crossed before that day comes. Nearly every biblical prophet also spoke of the Days of Tribulation, a time that culminates at a point when so few people will be left that a 'child can number them' [5]. The destruction leading to that condition will be brought about through a number of ways [6], but it is clear that the saints won't make it unless they gather. Joseph Smith said, "In addition to all temporal blessings, there is no other way for the Saints to be saved in these last days, than by gathering..." [7].

A Symbol of the Atonement

The Hebrew word for atonement can mean to cover. The Callout is a shadow of the Savior's atoning sacrifice, his compassion upon the family of Adam, and his power to protecting, enable, and indeed, to cover. Those who hear the Lord's voice through his servants, the prophets, will be protected as the children of Israel, who's angel of destruction passed by those who obeyed Moses' simple invitation to put lambs' blood over their doors; or those who would be healed from the lethal fiery serpents if they would merely cast their eyes upon the brazen serpent raised by Moses (see Alma 33:19-21). And yet, according to some visionary individuals, it appears there will be many who won't find deliverance by merely following the simple direction to gather and be called out.

But even more importantly than the assurance of temporal safety in these special prepared places, is the gradual elevation of spirituality in those who are faithful. The Abrahamic trials faced by the saints will have just the sanctifying effect needed to prepare them to inhabit the transfigured earth at the time of the Second Coming. Doctrine and Covenants Section 88 describes the laws that exist for inhabiting such a kingdom of glory. The dimmed light of this earth caused by its adulterous and murderous inhabitants is not a home fit for the King of Kings. It appears that only the removal of those evil-doers, and the increased righteousness of the remnant will bring the earth into the necessary level of light that is needed to welcome the Prince of Peace.

In summary, the Callout is a type and shadow of all of the redeeming, enabling, and covering powers of the Savior's atonement. To claim the blessings of The Callout, may we do that which has been told us for hundreds of years - hearken to the prophet. Put oil in our lamps, and be prepared. Live righteously. Prepare for the return of the Lord, the King of Kings (Revelation 19:16). I am confident that this special gathering of safety will occur, and I thank God for mercifully providing this small and simple means that is so layered in purpose and meaning, and the fulfillment of prophecy.

All sources in this post and more can be found below.

[1] **Missouri Myths** - Ensign, Apr. 1979

[2] • **Elder H. Aldridge** (Second Quorum of the Seventy) LDS Business College Devotional, February 8th, 2005. "We must both learn what these signs are and then identify them correctly when they occur. They can and will strengthen our faith in Christ and His prophets, if we know the scriptures. **Just as in the days of Noah, a way is already prepared for the escape of the Lord's elect Latter-Day Saints, if they are in tune with His prophets.**"

• **Joseph Smith** – The Teachings of the Prophet Joseph Smith, Section 2, P. 71. …. for without Zion, and a place of deliverance, we must fall; because the time is near when the sun will be darkened, and the moon turn to blood, and the stars fall from the heaven, and the earth reel to and fro. Then, if this is the case, and **if we are not sanctified and gathered to the places God has appointed, with all our former professions and our great love for the Bible, we must fall**; we cannot stand; we cannot be saved; for God will gather out his saints from the Gentiles, and then comes desolation and destruction, and none can escape except the pure in heart who are gathered.

• **Joseph Smith** DHC 4:272. "In addition to all temporal blessings, **there is no other way for the Saints to be saved in these last days, than by gathering….**"

• **James E. Talmage**, Conference Report, October 1921, p.188. "Great and grand as is this people, mighty as are the works that have been accomplished through the blessings of God through his servants in these days, there is too little real prayer among the Latter-day Saints, too many prayerless homes, and hence the spread of spiritual contagion among some of us. Thank the Lord not among many, relatively speaking. I have faith in my people, for I knew that they are the Lord's people, and I am proud to be one of them; but when the cry shall come, as come it shall: "**To your tents, O Israel**," for there are struggles ahead, the Lord knows where to find those who have been faithful."

• **President Howard W. Hunter**, "An Anchor to the Souls of Men," Ensign, Oct. 1993, 70 – "I promise you in the name of the Lord whose servant I am that God will always protect and care for his people. We will have our difficulties the way every generation and people have had difficulties. But with the gospel of Jesus Christ, you have every hope and promise and reassurance. **The Lord has power over his Saints and will always prepare places of peace,**

defense, and safety for his people. When we have faith in God we can hope for a better world-for us personally, and for all mankind."

• **Henry B. Eyring**, "Safety in Counsel" June 2008 First Presidency Message - "We are blessed to live in a time when the priesthood keys are on the earth. We are blessed to know where to look and how to listen for the voice that will fulfill the promise of the Lord that He will gather us to safety. I pray that we will have humble hearts, that we will listen, that we will pray, and that we will wait for the deliverance of the Lord that is sure to come as we are faithful."

• **Henry B. Eyring** – "Raise the Bar", January 2005; "…places of safety"

• **Revelation 18: 4** - And I heard another voice from heaven, saying, Come out of her, (Babylon) my people, that ye be not partakers of her sins , and that ye receive not of her plagues

• **Wilford Woodruff** – History of the Church, 6:26 - "… that the saints of God may have a place to flee to and stand in Holy Places while judgment works in the earth; that when the sword of God that is bathed in heaven falls upon Idumea, or the world, - when the Lord pleads with all flesh by sword and by fire, and the slain of the Lord are many, the Saints may escape these calamities by fleeing to the Places of Refuge, like Lot and Noah."

[3] **Dallin H. Oaks,** Spiritual Gifts, September 1986

[4]http://awlam-urim.blogspot.com/2015/03/march-15-2015-abrahamic-covenant.html

[5] **Isaiah 10: 18-19; 2 Nephi 20** – The destruction of Assyria is a type of the destruction of the wicked at the Second Coming— Few people will be left after the Lord comes again;

Isaiah 24: 6 – Therefore hath the curse devoured the earth, and they that dwell therein are desolate: therefore the inhabitants of the earth are burned, and few men left;

Orson Pratt, JD, Vol 20. June 23, 1878. "What, only a few persons to be converted, only a few to receive the true Gospel, and be prepared for the coming of the Bridegroom; only a few people to escape this awful desolation? So says the Prophet Isaiah; that is, few in comparison to the great and numerous population of our globe."

[6] **1 Nephi 14: 3** – That great pit which hath been digged for the destruction of men shall be filled by those who digged it, unto their utter destruction;

Doctrine and Covenants 88: 94 - And another angel shall sound his trump, saying: That great church, the mother of abominations… she is the tares of the earth; she is bound in bundles; her bands are made strong, no man can loose them; therefore, she is ready to be burned;

Doctrine and Covenants 43: 25-26 - …Behold, the day has come, when the cup of the wrath of mine indignation is full;

Mormon 8: 41 – The sword of vengeance hangeth over the wicked;

2 Nephi 6:18 – I will feed them that oppress thee with their own flesh;

1 Nephi 11: 36 – The fall of the great and spacious building was exceedingly great;

Doctrine and Covenants 29: 21 – And the great and abominable church…shall be cast down by devouring fire;

1 Nephi 22: 13-14 - The great and abominable church shall turn upon their own heads; war among themselves; shall be drunken with their own blood. Every nation which shall war against Israel shall fall into the pit which they digged to ensnare the people of the Lord. All that fight against Zion shall be destroyed.

[7] **Joseph Smith DHC 4:272**.

ADDITIONAL VOLUMES

The Julie Rowe Show consists of six volumes that will be released throughout 2018.

Volume Two

11. Young Adults in the Last Days
12. Impromptu Discussion on Prayer
13. What I See in the Midwest
14. How I Receive Revelation
15. Julie's Fortune and Fame
16. Keeping It Real with Julie
17. Julie's Witness of the Savior
18. Upcoming GTRF Initiatives
19. What I See in the Northeast U.S.
20. Different Types of Sin

Volume Three

21. What I See in the Southeast United States
22. Transitioning to the Church of the Firstborn
23. Worship and the Sabbath Day
24. Fearless
25. What I See in Canada and Mexico
26. The Message
27. Signs in the Heavens Part 2
28. Power in the Priesthood
29. New Jerusalem
30. Eric's Struggle with Julie's Message

Volume Four

31. Jewish Holidays and Heavenly Signs
32. Tribulations 101
33. Tribulations 102
34. Julie and the LDS Church
35. Missionaries Called Home
36. The Davidic Servant
37. Founding Fathers
38. Abrahamic Covenant and Cities of Light
39. My Witness of Jesus Christ
40. Prophets and Prophecy

Volume Five

41. Dates, Signs, Revelations, and NDEs
42. Sadducees and Pharisees
43. Condescension
44. Charity
45. Forgiveness
46. Fortitude
47. Accountability
48. Letting Go of the Outcome
49. Christmas 2017
50. Truth

Volume Six

51. Memories from Adam to Jacob
52. Memories from Joseph to Moses
53. Memories from Aaron to Nephi on the Tower
54. Memories from Mary Magdalene
55. Memories from Mary Magdalene Queen Isabella
56. Memories from Hawaiian Warrior to Sarah Goode
57. Memories from Ben Franklin to Anne Frank
58. Temple Worship
59. Transitions
60. Thy Kingdom Come

ABOUT THE AUTHORS

Julie Rowe

Julie and her husband Jeff have three beautiful children and live in the Midwest.

She was raised as a military dependent, and has lived in several different places: Utah, Texas, California, Washington state, New Jersey, Hawaii, Upstate New York, northern Virginia, Kansas, Arizona, and Heidelberg, Germany.

Julie received her Bachelor of Science degree from Brigham Young University in 1999, and her teaching certificate from the University of Saint Mary in 2010.

She loves camping and recreational activities with her family, and attending her children's athletic events and music concerts. She also enjoys spending time with extended family and friends.

She is an avid reader and loves learning about history, geography, science and a variety of other subjects. One of her favorite things in the whole world is to do family history work. She also enjoys meeting and talking to new people.

Julie has a passion for missionary work and a strong testimony of the importance of spreading the Good Word. She is very grateful for the tender mercies of the Lord, and has been a recipient of many. She is very grateful for the blessing and opportunity she has been given to share her story.

She is the author of three previous books: *A Greater Tomorrow, The Time Is Now,* and *From Tragedy to Destiny*.

She can be reached at **agreatertomorrow2014@gmail.com**

Eric J. Smith

Eric J. Smith works as a Geographic Information Systems consultant in east Idaho, and has operated his own business since 2009. On the side for a fun change of pace he teaches mapping classes as an Adjunct Faculty member in the History, Geography, and Political Science department of Brigham Young University Idaho.

He received his Bachelor of Science degree in University Studies from BYU Idaho in 2004, and then received his Master of Science degree in Geographic Information Science from Idaho State University in 2013.

For ten years he had a side hobby of mapping cemeteries, bringing a high degree of spatial accuracy to the cemetery mapping industry. His professional life often had a focus on emergency preparedness and disaster mitigation, and he was able to receive training at FEMA's National Emergency Training Center in Maryland with a focus on mapping.

In 2016 he was able to combine his personal and professional interests and started a 501c3 charitable organization called Mapping Hands Incorporated, focused on cemetery and disaster relief mapping.

Eric has researched and studied Judeo-Christian doctrines, studying Biblical Hebrew under Bruce Satterfield at BYU-Idaho. He operates a blog called "Doctrinal Essays" where he publishes his research and thoughts on meaningful topics.

In 2016 he teamed up with Spring Creek Books as an editor, seeking to gain experience in the writing industry. This ultimately led him to write Julie Rowe's biography, which will be released in 2018.

Eric loves his simplistic Idaho lifestyle. He enjoys the outdoors with his wife Melissa and five children, as well as woodwork, jazz music, and cooking. Eric would love to hear from his readers and can be contacted at **agreatertomorrow2014@gmail.com**